BETWEEN THE LAUGHS:

OUR GREATEST COMEDIANS TALK SERIOUSLY ABOUT COMEDY AND EACH OTHER

edited by
GARRY BERMAN

BETWEEN THE LAUGHS:
OUR GREATEST COMEDIANS TALK SERIOUSLY
ABOUT COMEDY AND EACH OTHER
©2012 GARRY BERMAN

ALL RIGHTS RESERVED.

No part of this book may be reproduced in any form or by any means, electronic, mechanical, digital, photocopying, or recording, except for in the inclusion of a review, without permission in writing from the publisher.

Published in the USA by:

BEARMANOR MEDIA
P.O. BOX 71426
ALBANY, GEORGIA 31708
www.BearManorMedia.com

ISBN-10: 1-59393-275-8 (alk. paper)
ISBN-13: 978-1-59393-275-6 (alk. paper)

Printed in the United States of America.

BOOK DESIGN AND LAYOUT BY VALERIE THOMPSON

TABLE OF CONTENTS

INTRODUCTION 1

I   COMEDY AS ART 3
               NO LAUGHING MATTER 5
               TO BE A NATURAL 6
               WHAT'S SO FUNNY? 9
               CREATING COMEDY 11
               TRIAL AND ERROR 13
               JEWISH COMEDIANS: WHY SO MANY? 16
               COMEDY IS TIMELESS...SOMETIMES 17

II   THE VAUDEVILLIANS 19

III   THE SILENT FILM COMEDIANS 29

IV   THE GOLDEN AGE OF TALKIES 37

V   THE RADIO SPECIALISTS 45

VI   THE WAR YEARS AND BEYOND 51
               THE DIRECTORS SPEAK 55

VII	THE TELEVISION LEGENDS 57
	THE SKETCH COMEDIANS 69
	THE LATE-NIGHT HOSTS 70

VIII	THE STAND-UP COMEDIANS 75
	WHAT DOES IT TAKE? 75
	WRITING JOKES 78
	WORKING ONSTAGE 80
	SHADES OF BLUE 83
	FLOP SWEAT 84
	THE GREEN-EYED MONSTER 86
	THE WANNABES 87
	THE BORSCH BELT/NIGHTCLUB COMICS 88
	THE 'NEW WAVE' COMEDIANS OF THE '50S 91
	THE '60S AND BEYOND 99
	THE BIG PAYOFF 105
	FROM STAND-UPS TO SITCOMS 107
	COMEDIANS FACE-TO-FACE 110

IX	COMEDIANS AS ACTORS 113

X	IN CLOSING... 119

BIBLIOGRAPHY 121

INDEX 127

INTRODUCTION

The past century has produced a finite number of special entertainers who, primarily through instinct but not without endless trial and error, have known how to make an audience laugh. And, among the best of these, no two comedians have gone about it in quite the same way. Each has found something unique within themselves that could be molded and shaped into a comic character and style. For instance, no comedian has ever presented himself to an audience in quite the way W.C. Fields did, just as no one has duplicated Buster Keaton's great stone face, or Groucho Marx's way of delivering an absurd pun. And yet these men as comedians had little in common with each other, and used vastly different ways to achieve their desired results. As Steve Allen said, "There is no one right way to make people laugh."

While we most often see our favorite comedians while they are actually in performance—be it in a film, on television, or doing a stand-up routine—there is another, and fascinating side to comedians that is revealed only when they aren't "on." The best of them are serious about their art, aware of their contemporaries and their predecessors, and know countless techniques to make an audience laugh. They also know what *not* to do to ensure success. Like magicians, they don't let us see the mechanics of their performances, and like magicians, can even play with the minds of their audiences. Unlike magicians, however—and thankfully so—comedians are more willing to reveal their methods once they leave the spotlight and the stage.

This quote book contains comments, observations, words of praise, and a few of derision, made by the greatest comedians, dating back to the turn of the 20th Century, as they speak candidly about comedy and each other. The general public has always been accustomed to hearing critics and show business observers offer their opinions of who is or isn't funny, and why. A few of those critics are included here, as are film directors and writers, but most of the comments are from the comedians themselves, giving us a glimpse of how they create their comedy, and what it's like to work in their profession. Some of the quotes are brief, comprising just a few words, while others are necessarily longer. Yet they all demonstrate how a handful of words can reveal much about the thoughts behind them, and about those expressing them. How did W.C. Fields feel about Charlie Chaplin? What did Buster Keaton think of Abbott & Costello? What did Jackie Gleason say about Buster Keaton? The answers are here, but there are no jokes to be found. Rather, there are words of admiration, jealousy, rivalry, and, above all, a love for the art of making people laugh.

Chapter 1
Comedy as Art

Milton Berle: Of course it's an art form. Absolutely, absolutely. But it's a delicate art form.

Jack Benny: Playing comedy is often as delicate an operation as taking apart the springs and wheels and levers of a fine Swiss watch—and putting them together again.

W. C. Fields: The funniest thing about comedy is that you never know why people laugh. I know *what* makes them laugh, but trying to get your hands on the *why* of it is like trying to pick an eel out of a tub of water.

Johnny Carson: I don't know what makes people laugh. I know devices that make people laugh, but I don't know *why* people laugh.

Shecky Green: I've been doing comedy a little over 50 years. I still don't know what makes people laugh.

Shelley Berman: I don't know what makes anybody funny or un-funny...I don't know what makes a comedian a comedian.

Ed Wynn: A comedian isn't a man who says funny things. A comedian is a man who says things funny.

Jerry Stiller: Creating laughter is an intimate act—it creates affection. The ugly toad becomes a handsome prince if he can make you laugh.

John Cleese: You always feel great affection for anyone who makes you laugh, even if they do so with an appalling persona, like W.C. Fields or Basil Fawlty.

Dorothy Parker: There are those who, in their pride and their innocence, dedicate their careers to writing humorous pieces. Poor dears, the world is stacked against them from the start, for everybody in it has the right to look at their work and say, 'I don't think that's funny.'

Ed Wynn: No comedian ever lived who pleased everybody, no matter how great he was, there was someone who thought he was not great.

Jan Murray: I must say, after all these years in this business, comedy to me is still mysterious. It cannot be defined. Everybody *tries* to define it...and still, the mystery remains.

Neil Simon: A joke is something someone else tells you, which is then passed on to someone else who hasn't heard it yet. No one knows where those jokes come from. *No one.* They are as difficult to trace as the day the universe was born.

E.B. White: Humor can be dissected, as a frog can, but the thing dies in the process and the innards are discouraging to any but the pure scientific mind.

Steve Allen: Analytical knowledge about humor does not detract from and may actually enhance its enjoyment...One should not be afraid, therefore, of learning the secrets of the magicians of comedy. You will still laugh. And the essential mystery will forever elude you.

Bob Newhart: The closer you get to understanding humor, the more you begin to lose your sense of humor.

Steve Martin: The day you start analyzing humor is the day you cease to be funny. I think I'd rather be funny.

Groucho Marx: I gave up trying to find out why people are funny a long, long time ago.

No Laughing Matter

Buddy Hackett: What funny is, is relief from pain.

W. C. Fields: To understand comedy, to know what laughs are made of, one must suffer. Every laugh is built on heartaches, sometimes tears.

Ed Wynn: In all true comedy, there must be an undercurrent of pathos; and the pathos can only come from the comedian's intimate acquaintanceship with the heartbreaks, the misery, and the elemental sadness of life.

Alan King: In one way or another, comedy is a response to adversity. Most comedians have gone through some form of hardship in their early lives.

Milton Berle: Steve Allen thinks comedy is—tragedy plus time. I'll accept that. In the late twenties, a young redheaded kid named Skelton believed that comedy was—getting even. I'll buy that definition too.

Jackie Gleason: Comedy without pathos is like sitting down to a meal without bread.

Lenny Bruce: All my humor is based on destruction and despair.

Phyllis Diller: Comedy is tragedy revisited.

Steve Martin: Comedy looks easy. Drama looks hard.

Jerry Lewis: Comedy is a man in trouble, and comedians react to it in different ways. Chaplin was a ballet dancer—he'd dance through trouble. Keaton became part of a well-oiled machine—he'd slip easily through a small opening. I'd have my arms outstretched and get stuck.

Sid Caesar: There is a fine line between laughter and tears. When you laugh too hard, you start to cry. When you cry too hard, you start to laugh. When someone doesn't know whether to laugh or cry, your comedy is working.

To Be A Natural

Neil Simon: No one has yet to determine, to my satisfaction, what elements of nature, genetics, and environment have to combine to form a man or woman with a keen sense of humor.

CAROL BURNETT: If you're naturally funny, it will come out. I don't think any amount of training is going to make someone funny.

JERRY LEWIS: "In the bones" funny is a gift. You're either born with it or you're not. Gleason had it. Milton Berle had it. Sid Caesar and Stan Laurel had it. Charlie Chaplin had more of it than anyone else...Dean [Martin] had it too, yet he never understood the depth of his own skill.

RODNEY DANGERFIELD: I've learned over the years that when you get to know the "naturals," you find that they work very hard at their craft.

BERT WILLIAMS: I do not believe there is any such thing as innate humor. It has to be developed by hard work and study, just as every other human quality. I have studied it all my life, unconsciously during my floundering years, and consciously as soon as I began to get next to myself. It is a study that I shall never get to the end of, and a work that never stops, except when I am asleep.

JACKIE GLEASON: There are non-performers who are very funny, but they don't have the chutzpah to stand on the stage and say, 'I'm funny—put that camera on me, I'll make you laugh.' I've met hundreds of guys at cocktail parties who are funnier than I am, but they don't have that ego...I'm not conceited. I *know* I'm good. Conceit is when you're *not* good and you think you are.

ROBIN WILLIAMS: Can I call myself a genius? N-o-o-o! I can say I get flashes once in a while. These riffs that run through you and you know it's something you've never done before, and that's great.

JOHN CANDY: There's a name for people like me. I think whore is the word. I'll be funny for a price.

JACK BENNY ON GEORGE BURNS:
I never can make George Burns laugh. Never! He never laughs at me. And I laugh at him all the time. It drives me crazy.

GEORGE BURNS ON JACK BENNY:
Jack always tried to set me up for a laugh. Like the time Gracie and I arrived in Minneapolis and checked in at Jack's hotel. I called him and told him I was coming up. Jack said, "Don't come up for two minutes." I knew right away he was setting me up. So when I got up there, sent the maid into his room ahead of me. Sure enough, he was standing on the bed, naked, with a flower in one hand and a pitcher of water in the other.

PHYLLIS DILLER ON GROUCHO MARX:
Groucho's delivery, and the way he lays a line out: That's where you study comedy. He could take a line and people would laugh. If somebody else said it, there wouldn't be a laugh. Now we're working with attitude, plus that cigar and those eyes. It's looking at this embodied attitude. He's a legend in his own time.

LUCILLE BALL: I can do funny things other people write down...but I don't *think* funny.

Peter Sellers: [I have] absolutely no personality at all. I am a chameleon. When I am not playing a role, I am nobody.

What's So Funny?

Soupy Sales: If a person falls down and he doesn't get up, it isn't funny, but if a person falls down and he gets up, it is funny.

Paul Rodriguez: Comedy is when you see an old woman slip and fall on a banana peel. Tragedy is if that old woman is your mother.

Mel Brooks: Tragedy is if I cut my finger. Comedy is if you walk into an open sewer and die.

Bert Williams: The sight of other people in trouble is nearly always funny. This is human nature. If you will observe your own conduct whenever you see a friend falling down on the street, you will find that nine times out of ten your first impulse is to laugh and your second is to run and help him get up. To be polite you will dust off his clothes and ask him if he has hurt himself. But when it is all over you cannot resist telling him how funny he looked when he was falling.

W.C. Fields: It is funnier to bend things than to break them—bend the fenders on a car in a comedy wreck, don't tear them off. In my golf game, which I have doing for years, at first I swung at the ball and broke the club. Now I bend it at a right angle. If one comedian hits another over the head with a crowbar, the crowbar should bend, not break. In legitimate drama, the hero breaks his sword, and it is dramatic, In comedy, the sword bends, and stays bent.

ROSCOE "FATTY" ARBUCKLE: If I didn't do anything but weigh 320 pounds and wear queer clothes I might get six laughs. In a half-hour picture-play I've got to get sixty or go out of business.

JONATHAN WINTERS: You can be funny without making it hokey. I pray to God that we're past the pie-throwing phase, and yet—I'm almost contradicting myself—I can still truthfully say that I laugh at Laurel and Hardy.

PAUL REISER: I like to consider myself a clever man. A not-unwitty man. A person who appreciates sophistication, subtlety, and nuance. And yet, I must admit that to me, nothing is funnier than a person getting hit on the head. Not to the point of injury, of course. But a nice thwack to the back of the skull? Nothing funnier. If it makes a funny noise, even better.

DAN AYKROYD: Some things are always going to make people laugh. In Neanderthal times, people probably laughed at jokes about burning themselves with fire and how funny their mates looked. We're laughing at the same things today—the things in our lives, human behavior.

JUDY GOLD: Anything that's taboo…If you say what people are thinking but are too afraid to say, it's funny. It's the truth. The truth is funny.

Creating Comedy

ALAN KING: Genius is not required in comedy. Except maybe in the case of Charlie Chaplin.

ERNIE KOVACS: My greatest pleasure is to sit at a typewriter with a sheaf of blank paper and start putting down ideas.

RAY ROMANO: It's hard to sit and write jokes and know it's going to work. The way I do it is I think of a funny premise, but you don't know exactly the form it's gonna take. I have a vague outline in my mind of the points I want to hit, and I say it to the audience, and you hear what's funny and what's not, and the audience helps you write it, just by trial and error.

STEVE ALLEN: Almost all comedians specialize. Some are good only in sketches and do not perform stand-up at all. Others, such as Jonathan Winters and Robin Williams, are spontaneously creative, whereas Bob Hope never is, and yet is still the most successful comedian of our time.

JAY LENO: I have no interest in thinking about [comedy]. I have no books about comedy. Walk around my house, you'd have a hard time figuring out what I do for a living...I don't have masks of comedy and tragedy, or Ed Wynn's hat on a hook. When you start thinking about comedy, you become a humorist or a satirist, and eventually you're out of business.

FANNY BRICE: Some comedians work out every detail of their business in putting over a song or an act, and I think it is a most admirable method, because it relieves one of the tyranny of moods. But I can't do it. My comedy, to be successful, must be spontaneous. Whenever it isn't, the feel of the audience tells me so and I throw out that particular piece of business and work out something else to use in its stead.

MOE HOWARD: Our three rules for working were watch, listen and plan. We watched the tempo of the act, listened to the other member when one was in the spotlight, and planned our routines. There was a lot more to it than just going up and telling funny stories and smacking each other around. We checked the slapstick carefully in order not to overdo it. If comedy goes on too long, the audience begins to think about it. We aimed not to give anyone time to think.

LARRY FINE: I think our comedy speaks for itself. It can't be described. You have to see it to believe it, 'cause we didn't pull any punches. I say "we"—Moe didn't pull any punches. When he hit, he hit. What you see is what we got! And many a time, we didn't even use sound effects.

CHEVY CHASE: My outlook, my comic delivery, everything about what I do is physical. I just make people laugh. It's not difficult. If all I did was write political humor and do stand-up work, it might be more difficult. If I were Mort Sahl it might be difficult.

W. C. Fields: I ad-lib most of my dialogue and have for years. If I did remember my lines, it would be too bad for me.

Stan Laurel: The derby hat has always seemed to be part of a comic's makeup for as far back as I can remember. I'm sure that's why Chaplin wore one...[Derbies] gave us something we felt these two characters needed—a kind of phony dignity. There's nothing funnier than a guy being dignified and dumb.

Oliver Hardy: I like to get a good reaction just the way any comedian does, but I have never really worked hard in the creation department. After all, just doing the gags is hard enough work, especially if you've taken as many falls and been dumped in as many mudholes as I have. I think I've earned my money.

Trial and Error

Groucho Marx: I believe all comedians arrive by trial and error. This was certainly true in the old days of vaudeville, and I'm sure it's true today...If the comic was inventive, he would gradually discard the stolen jokes and the ones that died and try out some of his own. In time, if he was any good, he would emerge from the routine character he had started with and evolve into a distinct personality of his own. This has been my experience...and I believe this has been true of most of the other comedians.

Jack Benny: To do a single [act] I would have to talk as well as play the fiddle. Where would I get the words? I wasn't rich enough to buy an act from a professional gag writer so I had to make one up myself. I figured out new jokes. I borrowed some. I stole some. My new act was Ben K. Benny: Fiddle Funology. I worked on it in front of a mirror by myself for two weeks. I paced it, I timed it, I chose the numbers.

W.C. FIELDS: Of course, [my first] act was a rough affair. I had no routine except as to the tricks. My comedy business was all dragged in as it occurred to me. I did whatever I thought would appear funny. If I remembered what had gone well at the last performance I worked it in, but generally I didn't remember.

GEORGE BURNS: When we first started, I had all the funny jokes and Gracie had the straight stuff, but even her straight lines got laughs. She had a funny delivery…It took a good year to get her into character. That doesn't mean it took a year to do a good act, but it took a year to get the wrong words out of Gracie's mouth…I wasn't good for a lot of years. I was a bad straight man. My job was not too attractive.

MAE WEST: Audiences have always been pleased by what I do, and I have always been doing the same basic thing, with different trimmings. I didn't recognize what I did myself at that time. I didn't know what it was I had. It wasn't until much later that anyone, including myself, realized that it was the force of an extraordinary sex-personality that made quite harmless lines and mannerisms seem suggestive. It wasn't what I did, but how I did it. It wasn't what I said, but how I said it; and how I looked when I did it and said it. I had evolved into a symbol and didn't know it.

MILTON BERLE: I copied my style from a great comic, Ted Healy. I patterned myself after Healy, with the hat turned up in front and the collegiate look. I was the brash, flippant, wise guy, smart-ass type. I created myself just through guts and nerve.

PHYLLIS DILLER: I had a beautiful figure, like Miss America. I never had the face, no, but the shape, yes. I wanted to make body jokes. So I had to hide it...All those feathers, beads, the fright wigs...It got laughs. Comedy is about being a loser. It's a hostile act.

JIM CARREY: One day...I decided to change my act—I wanted to stop doing my impressions and start being myself onstage. Well, things got pretty weird for a while after that. And by "weird" I mean that I was bombing night after night. But I stuck with it, mainly because I could always hear Rodney [Dangerfield] laughing in the wings.

LUCILLE BALL: I took the slapstick parts the other starlets spurned, and never whined about the siphon water and pies in the face. I considered myself lucky to be paid while still learning a business I adored.

HARPO MARX: I simply couldn't outtalk Groucho or Chico, and it was ridiculous for me to try. It was a cruel blow to my pride nevertheless...I went silent. I never uttered another word, on stage or in front of a camera, as a Marx Brother.

BUSTER KEATON: A few fan letters to Roscoe [Arbuckle] asked why the little man in his pictures never smiled. We had been unaware of it. We looked at three two-reelers we'd done together and found it to be true. Later just for fun I tried smiling at the end of one picture. The preview audience hated it and hooted the scene. After that I never smiled again on stage, screen, or TV.

THE JEWISH COMEDIANS: WHY SO MANY?

ALAN KING: On the road, I learned about prejudice. It wasn't only people of color who were discriminated against; I heard people refer to me as "that Jew comic," and for a while, in my act, I tried to be more white bread, more Waspy. It didn't work, it wasn't me. I finally said, Screw it, and after that, I wore my Jewishness like a badge of honor.

CARL REINER: Jack Benny, George Burns, Sid Caesar, Milton Berle, nobody ever said they were Jewish, but the Jews knew they were Jewish. The rest of the country didn't. We knew Benny was Benny Kubelsky, Milton Berle was Milton Berlinger. The Jews knew. The Jews were always happy to know which famous people were. There was a game we'd play: "Do you think he's Jewish?"

ED WYNN: The Jews are the only mass of people who

love to hear jokes about themselves...who can laugh at themselves. Though I never experienced any persecution. I think so many comedians being Jewish...is an outlet. Something that never happened with generations gone.

JACKIE MASON: People take different tacks to compensate for their misery. One person kills to compensate. One person fights back. One person laughs at himself. And that's the tradition of the Jew. The history of the Jew is enacted in my own life. It's traditional that the Jew becomes either a comedian or a scholar.

GROUCHO MARX: We Marx Brothers never denied our Jewishness. We simply didn't use it. We could have safely fallen back on the Yiddish theater, making secure careers for ourselves. But our act was designed from the start to have a broad appeal. If, because of Chico, a segment of the audience thought we were Italian, let them. Then they could admire my proficiency with a German accent.

Comedy Is Timeless...Sometimes

ED WYNN: The style of comedy has changed, like the style of music or the style of clothes.

JOAN RIVERS: Comedy does not change. We just dress it up differently. Men and women, our bodies, does money matter or doesn't it—I'm so ugly that...these themes are still universal themes.

Dan Rowan: No new jokes? Of course there are new jokes. It may be true that every new joke is a switch or a twist on an old joke, but as the old burlesque comic once said, "A joke is old only if you've heard it."

Steve Allen: Humor is a fragile thing and little of it keeps well over the years. Even Shakespeare's comedies would no longer be performed did they depend solely on their humor content.

Steve Martin: Unlike as in most of the arts, greatness in comedy is not necessarily judged by its ability to transcend generations. Comedy is designed to make people laugh now, not three generations later....But just because it isn't funny now doesn't mean it wasn't funny then.

Harold Lloyd: Principles of comedy persist from generation to generation. It is true that some jokes that made our grandparents laugh do not seem especially funny to us. But on the other hand, many of the same joke situations that convulsed us today—on the screen, radio or television—also made our grandparents and their grandparents before them rock and roll with laughter.

Bill Murray: There are examples of people who lasted and were really funny at the end. I think George Burns was funny all the way. I think Jack Benny was funny all the way. There are other guys I could name who haven't been funny for a while and are still working.

Chapter 2
The Vaudevillians

Fred Allen: You could be ignorant and be a star. You could be a moron and be wealthy. The elements that went to make up vaudeville were combed from the jungles, the four corners of the world, the intelligentsia and the subnormal...Vaudeville asked only that you own an animal or an instrument, or have a minimum of talent or a maximum of nerve. With these dubious assets vaudeville offered fame and riches. It was up to you.

Harpo Marx: Should you ever hear an old-time vaudevillian talk about 'the wonderful, golden day of one-night stands,' buy him another drink, but don't believe a word he's saying. He's lying through his teeth.

Henny Youngman: Looking back from today, you almost can't believe these dialect comics actually were allowed to perform. Believe me, you haven't seen racism or anti-Semitism until you've seen it performed by a comic wearing blackface or a prop nose. And yet these guys were among the most popular of all vaudeville performers.

Harpo Marx: If an audience didn't like us we had no trouble finding it out. We were pelted with sticks, bricks, spitballs, cigar butts, peach pits and chewed-out stalks of sugar cane. We took all this without flinching—until [our mother] Minnie gave us the high-sign that she'd collected our share of the receipts. Then we started throwing the stuff back at the audience, and ran like hell for the railroad station the second the curtain came down.

MILTON BERLE: In the days of vaudeville, it wasn't uncommon for a performer to "borrow" a joke from another performer. Etiquette demanded only that the borrower add to the joke to make it his own.

FRED ALLEN: Comedy acts were always the targets of the pirates. If a comedian was original and wrote his own material, or if he frequently bought new routines and songs to keep his act up to date, he soon found that other comedians were stealing parts of his act. For many years performers had no way to protect their gags, parodies, or bits of business. Copyright laws were ignored, and good gags spread like bad news.

GROUCHO MARX ON CHAPLIN:
We were playing in Canada, and so was Chaplin...I took a walk and I passed this dump theatre, the Sullivan-Considine. I heard the most tremendous roar of laughter, and I paid my ten cents and went in and there was a little guy on the stage, and he was walking around kinda funny. It was Chaplin. It was the greatest act I'd ever seen. All pantomime...I went back to the hotel and told my brothers what a real comedian was.

EDDIE CANTOR ON ED WYNN:
"The Perfect Fool" for more than a half-century. His lisp, his hands, his familiar chuckle, his good clean fun for the whole family, his adherence to the rule that jokes obscene should not be heard, stamps him as the stage comedian of the century.

GROUCHO MARX ON ED WYNN:
Friday night [I saw] the Ed Wynn show. Utterly delightful, a master comic, not a dirty line or joke in the entire two and a half hours.

EDDIE CANTOR ON WILL ROGERS:
He'd added a monologue to his [rope trick] act and he wasn't satisfied to joke, the jokes must have substance. Every morning he read the papers, the *Morning World*, the *New York Times*, the *American*, the *Tribune*. Then he'd sit down at his little portable typewriter and peck out his commentaries on the news. He'd never had much education...but he had a built-in shrewdness and he worked at it, edited it, until it became 99.9 per cent pure wisdom.

EDDIE CANTOR:
W.C. Fields, Will Rogers and I were in the 'Follies' of 1919. Would you believe it, not one of us would try a piece of business or a gag without consulting the other two? It was a kind of schooling.

GEORGE BURNS ON EDDIE CANTOR:
[He] had more energy than any performer who ever appeared on the stage. Maybe he didn't sing so well, and he wasn't a great

dancer, and most of his jokes really weren't that funny, but he did so much so fast that the audience didn't have time to notice. Slow motion instant replay would have killed Cantor's career.

MILTON BERLE ON EDDIE CANTOR:
Eddie Cantor had to fight for his laughs. Unlike some comedians who are ready to garner laughter a minute after birth, Cantor wasn't born a funny man...He had a desire to be funny, the urge to provoke laughter. The equipment was missing. He wished himself into comedy...Many comedians need writers, but Cantor NEEDED writers.

CHICO MARX ON EDDIE CANTOR:
Eddie's a great performer. He's not really a funny man, but he's a great performer.

JACK CARTER ON MILTON BERLE:
With a doubt Milton Berle was the biggest influence in my comedy life. As a kid, just to watch him at the Paramount Theater in New York firing off those rapid one-liners, quick asides, topical shtick was great.

EDDIE CANTOR ON BERT WILLIAMS:
The best negro comedian to trod the boards. The best teacher I ever had...I studied his extraordinary powers as a pantomimist, his incomparable way with an audience—manipulating their emotions as if they were puppets on strings.

W. C. FIELDS ON BERT WILLIAMS:
He was the funniest man I ever saw...and the saddest man I ever met.

GROUCHO MARX ON W. C. FIELDS:
> He was a tough guy. He was doing his juggling act, and there was a pool table on the stage, because he used to do funny stuff with a pool table, and Ed Wynn was also on the show. So Wynn used to get under the pool table, and while Fields was doing his stuff, Wynn would stick his head out and make funny faces. One day Fields caught him doing this and when Wynn stuck his out from under the table, Fields was standing there with a pool cue and he hit Wynn on the head and knocked him unconscious. He was a funny guy, but he didn't want anybody to interfere with his act. Or to upstage him.

SID CAESAR ON W.C. FIELDS:
> Fields' work taught me the essence of comic timing...I learned how to make a scene larger or smaller, how to grow and develop a laugh through using my body and contorting and manipulating my facial expressions.

ORSON WELLES ON W.C. FIELDS:
> If you can believe such a thing, [he] was even funnier on the stage. Bill Fields only had to cross the room, you know, and I'd be retching with laughter.

W.C. FIELDS ON FANNY BRICE:
> Comical dancer, comedienne, did burlesque dances, sang character songs in Yiddish and other dialects. She was a fine dramatic actress, believe it or prove your ignorance.

JACK BENNY ON THE MARX BROTHERS:
> When they got through with their act, that crazy act, no comedian could follow them, particularly a quiet comedian like myself.

W.C. FIELDS ON THE MARX BROS:
> Never saw so much nepotism or such hilarious laughter in one act in my life. The only act I could never follow. I told the theatre manager I broke my wrist and quit.

BILLY WILDER ON THE MARX. BROS:
> The Marx Brothers were at their best against a very serious, pompous background. They were very good in *A Night At The Opera* because it's very pompous, the opera. They were also quite good at the race track, in *A Day At The Races*. But other things they did, there were not so good because there was nothing to poke at...But Groucho was a genius, absolutely a fabulous, fabulous man.

EDDIE CANTOR ON GROUCHO MARX:
> An astounding ad-libber, every other comedian can tell you that Groucho can wither you with one line.

CHEVY CHASE ON GROUCHO MARX:
> The Marx Brothers and particularly Groucho, had a profound effect on the lives of all people with a sense of humor. For me Groucho was a major influence.

DICK CAVETT ON GROUCHO MARX:
> There is a frustrating sense in which Groucho is not convinced of his greatness and is in need of proof that he is adored, and this should not be.

BOB HOPE ON GROUCHO MARX:

Seldom is the word 'genius' used to describe a comedian, especially by another comedian, but to me Julius (Groucho) Marx was just that. The grease moustache, the huge cigar, the loping walk, the utter disregard for female sensitivities, and the puncturing of all the phonies in the entire world set Groucho and his style apart from every other ordinary mortal. He was outrageous, brilliant, savage, insulting, and hilarious at the same time...Groucho's style made it almost impossible to top him, so very wisely I didn't try.

JACK PAAR ON GROUCHO MARX:

It was always good for the program to have Groucho Marx as a guest, but to tell you the truth, he bored me. You could not have a conversation with him—at least I never could—on or off the stage. It was a tiresome monologue, consisting mostly of puns. If anyone ever needed editing, it was Groucho...[He] was not, as you would assume, a favorite among his peers. He was neither known for his wit nor his kindness.

ALEXANDER WOOLLCOTT ON HARPO MARX:

Surely there should be dancing in the streets when a great clown comic comes to town, and this man is a great clown...Harpo Marx, so styled, oddly enough, because he plays the harp, says never a word from first to last, but when by merely leaning against one's brother one can seem richly and irresistibly amusing why should one speak?

JACK PAAR ON GEORGE JESSEL:
>Jessel had a funny, flowery turn of phrase and adventures that convulsed his peers. If I ever saw a crowed gathering around a certain table, it always meant George was the centerpiece.

THE *NEW YORK TIMES* (JULY 17, 1928):
>Jessel is, beyond question, a smart and vaudeville-wise entertainer and he had things pretty much his way yesterday. Most of his comedy is funny—especially some of the lines that he employs in a telephone speech with his mother—and he knows how to dispense the sort of elementary sentiment that brings direct returns from his auditors. He is, in sum, a showman, and his act is deservedly among the played-up items of the bill.

GEORGE BURNS ON GRACIE ALLEN:
>I just timed the jokes for Gracie...[her] sense of concentration was so marvelous that she didn't know there was an audience.

BOB HOPE ON BURNS & ALLEN:
>George was very much an equal partner in the act; his art of submerging himself to Gracie's comic talent was just that, an art.

STEVE ALLEN ON GEORGE BURNS:
>George's power to amuse is remarkable considering the minimum of effort he has always made.

ALAN KING ON BERT LAHR:
>A devotee of other comedians, I watched everybody work. I watched the nightclub

stars and I watched the big stage comedians, Frank Fay, Jimmy Savo, Bobby Clark, and my all-time favorite, Bert Lahr. [He] was a man of massive comedic talents.

NEIL SIMON ON BERT LAHR:
Bert Lahr [was] one of the funniest men who ever lived. [He] was a compulsive worrier who never thought his performance was good enough...He valued a laugh onstage as much as a collector valued a Renoir in his study, and anyone who came close to stealing it would pay the direst penalty.

MILTON BERLE ON BERT LAHR:
Bert Lahr was a great comedian. We all know that. But he was a nervous, moody man, a comedian who gave up on an audience too quickly. If he didn't get a laugh in the first twenty seconds, that was it.

HENNY YOUNGMAN ON MILTON BERLE:
I had some jokes I was selling, ten for a dime. So I gave Milton ten jokes, and he laughed. He said, 'I like these, and I like you.' And he started coming around every day, he'd spend a little time with me in between shows, and he became my guru.

JACK BENNY ON FRED ALLEN:
I admired Fred Allen—for his generous nature as a person and for his sharp and cutting wit as a comedian...In vaudeville, [his] was one of the smartest acts of its time. He was always miles ahead of most other performers.

ALAN KING ON GROUCHO, JESSEL:
At Hillcrest [Country Club], I just sat and listened to the big boys. They were funny, and they knew they were funny; it was fireworks, each of them trying to outdo the others. Groucho never stopped (if you could tell forty jokes, three of them are bound to work) but even Groucho shut up when Jessel was forth. Jack [Benny] was the only relatively quite one; offstage, he was an introverted man.

ALAN KING: Today, there are a lot of wonderful young comedians who make me laugh, but the ones I like have a sense of history and tradition. Richard Pryor, Billy Crystal, Robin Williams, they don't get into bed at night saying, 'Today, I invented show business."

FRED ALLEN: Portland and I started doing a vaudeville act together shortly after we were married. In vaudeville, when a comedian married he immediately put his wife in the act. The wife didn't have to have any talent. It was economic strategy. With a double act a comedian could get a salary increase from the booking office. The additional money would pay for his wife's wardrobe, her railroad fares and the extra hotel expenses.

GEORGE BURNS: Vaudeville didn't just drop dead, it faded slowly, like applause after a second encore.

Chapter 3
The Silent Film Comedians

Buster Keaton: Neither Chaplin, Harold Lloyd or myself ever had a script. That sounds impossible to anybody in the picture business today. We never thought of writing a script. Somebody would always come up with a start. We'd say, that's funny, that's a good start. We want to know the finish, right then and there. There's nothing to work toward but the finish.. The middle we can always take care of. That's easy.

Roscoe "Fatty" Arbuckle: In the first place, I make up my own plays. I don't write them. I make them up as I go along. I have a general idea in my head when we begin, but I don't have a written scenario or even a synopsis. I try out every scene I can think of, working out he business by actually rehearsing it. And all the time I'm rehearsing out here I'm trying to devise funny little twists that will get a laugh...By the time I'm through I have about 15,000 feet of film—and all I need is 2,000 feet. I've got to skin the cream off that milk. I go over all the films and pick out the best scenes. Then is the time I write the story. I make out the scenario from the scenes I intend to use.

BUSTER KEATON ON ROSCOE "FATTY" ARBUCKLE:
> The longer I worked with Roscoe the more I liked him…He took falls no man his weight ever attempted, had a wonderful mind for action gags, which he could devise on the spot…I could not have found a better-natured man to teach me the movie business, or a more knowledgeable one. We never had an argument.

LOUELLA PARSONS ON ARBUCKLE:
> Everything a comedian should be is present in "Fatty." He radiates good nature, cheerfulness and a pleasant day…To the surprise of all not a sound emanated from the Arbuckle sets. Without exception they were amazed at the seriousness of the comedians and the strict attention paid to the slightest detail by "Fatty" who not only acts, but writes, cuts and directs his own pictures.

STAN LAUREL:
> We all thought Charlie was a fool for leaving the superiority of the stage for the doubtful medium of moving pictures. Charlie was getting $60.00 a week of which he was sure, and he was a great hit as the silk-hatted, red-nosed drunk in the theatre box, who interrupted our performance every evening.

CHARLIE CHAPLIN:
> I was not terribly enthusiastic about the Keystone type of comedy, but I realized their publicity value. A year at that racket and I could return to vaudeville an international star. Besides, it would mean a new life and a pleasant environment

KEATON ON CHAPLIN'S LITTLE TRAMP CHARACTER:
...A bum with a bum's philosophy...He would steal if he got the chance. My little fellow was a workingman and honest.

HARPO MARX ON CHAPLIN:
Charlie Chaplin was my idea of comic genius. I would watch a Chaplin picture four, five, or six times over. What an artist!

W.C. FIELDS ON CHAPLIN:
That Goddamed ballet dancer.

DAN AYKROYD ON CHARLIE CHAPLIN:
I saw all his movies when I was a kid. My dad would rent them and show them on a bed sheet in the basement. But I preferred the Keystone Cops, Laurel and Hardy, and Buster Keaton.

STAN LAUREL ON CHARLIE CHAPLIN:
The difference between Charlie an all the rest of us—with only one exception, Buster Keaton—was that he just absolutely refused to do anything but the best. To get the best he worked harder than anyone I know.

FIELDS ON CHAPLIN: I hope Chaplin's picture [*The Great Dictator*] is as bad as the critics say it is.

ALBERT BROOKS ON CHAPLIN:
I was never a huge Chaplin fan. The main reason was the movie was always speeded up and I never knew what he could really do. If I went to the bathroom at that speed, I would be hysterical. I grew up loving Laurel & Hardy.

JERRY LEWIS ON CHAPLIN:
Discussing Chaplin's genius would be like measuring the ocean with a cup.

ORSON WELLES ON CHAPLIN:
Chaplin's a great artist—there can't be any argument about that. It's just that he seldom makes the corners of my mouth move up. I find him easy to admire and hard to laugh at.

BENNY HILL ON CHAPLIN:
I get a tremendous kick from watching people like Charles Chaplin and Jacques Tati. Slowing down some of the classic scenes from *City Lights* and *The Gold Rush* shows how much attention to detail went into Chaplin's seemingly straightforward slapstick routines.

BUSTER KEATON:
I've always tried to challenge the imagination of my audience. I always challenged them to outguess me, and then I'd double-cross them.

STAN LAUREL ON BUSTER KEATON:
One of the reasons why I love Buster so much is because he lives comedy as well as practices it. Some of his things are better than Chaplin's.

WOODY ALLEN ON CHAPLIN/KEATON:
I think Keaton was a better filmmaker, but Chaplin was the funnier man.

JACKIE GLEASON ON CHAPLIN/KEATON:
Chaplin had one character—the little tramp—and he stuck with it to great critical

acclaim and financial success, but for sheer comic creativity, he wasn't in the same league with Buster Keaton.

JAMES AGEE ON KEATON:
Keaton worked strictly for laughs, but his work came from so far inside a curious and original spirit that he achieved a great deal besides, especially in his feature-length comedies...He was the only major comedian who kept sentiment almost entirely out of his work, and he brought pure physical comedy to its greatest heights.

RED SKELTON ON BUSTER KEATON:
My teacher was Buster Keaton. He was working for MGM when I made my debut at that studio. Keaton told me over and over, 'Always care for your props.'

MEL BROOKS ON BUSTER KEATON:
I don't think he was a genius. Einstein was a genius. Buster Keaton was *astonishing*. I've never seen any human being able to perform as brilliantly and gracefully with such unusually gifted timing. There was only one Keaton.

ORSON WELLES ON BUSTER KEATON:
Keaton was beyond all praise...a very great artist, and one of the most beautiful men I ever saw on the screen. He was also a superb director. In the last analysis, nobody came near him.

TERRY JONES ON BUSTER KEATON:
My big hero is Buster Keaton because he made comedy look beautiful; he took it

seriously. He didn't say, 'Oh, it's comedy, so we don't need to bother about the way it looks."

OLIVER HARDY ON LARRY SEMON:
He was a good comedian—a very good acrobatic comedian—and he always knew a good gag when he saw one. He used to have a little black book that he'd keep in his back trouser pocket. That little book was worth thousands and thousands of dollars because he always kept all his comedy ideas in it. I never saw anyone work harder at making a gag work out, except maybe Stan.

BUSTER KEATON ON LARRY SEMON:
Chaplin, Lloyd and myself just couldn't make two-reelers as packed with laughs as Larry's.

HAROLD LLOYD:
We always called the "Glasses" character, the character with the spectacles…When I started that character, it gave me an entirely different viewpoint. It made my romantic ends in the picture very believable, where most the contemporaries I worked with, and myself before—when I was doing comedy clothes and big shoes and everything—I had to have a girl then who was almost as screwy as I was, in order to make them believe that you could get the girl.

LEO MCCAREY ON HAROLD LLOYD:
He was a great judge of comedy values—and therein lay his secret of success: it was very apparent that he was a veritable genius.

HAL ROACH ON HAROLD LLOYD:
>Harold Lloyd was not a comedian, but he was one of the best actors around. He *played* a comedian.

JAMES AGEE ON HAROLD LLOYD:
>If great comedy must involve something beyond laughter, Lloyd was not a great comedian. If plain laughter is any criterion—and it is a healthy counterbalance to the other—few people have equaled him, and nobody has ever beaten him.

LEO MCCAREY ON CHARLEY CHASE:
>I had so many ideas for gags that [Hal Roach] gave me an actor named Charley Chase and he let me direct him. I was fortunate enough to draw a very clever fellow. He was a big help too me and I hope that I reciprocated to him. And our pictures were extremely successful.

KEATON ON MACK SENNETT:
>The mystery is how this seemingly humorless man managed to find and develop more first-rate comic talent than anyone else in the history of show business.

BILLY CRYSTAL ON HAL ROACH:
>This is the guy who said to Laurel & Hardy, 'You'd be good together!' This is the guy who gave us Our Gang, this is a guy who was very responsible for comedy on film.

STAN LAUREL (ON A SCHOLARLY ASSESSMENT OF CHAPLIN):
>That kind of junk annoys the hell out of me. What people like that don't understand

and never will understand is that what we were trying to do was to make people laugh in as many ways was we could, without trying to prove a point or show the world its troubles or get into some deep meaning. Why the hell do you have to explain why a thing is funny? We were trying to do a very simple thing, give people some laughs, and that's *all* we were trying to do.

Chapter 4
The Golden Age of Talkies

Chaplin: *Modern Times* was a great success...The whole of Hollywood had deserted silent pictures and I was the only one left. I had been lucky so far, but to continue with a feeling that the art of pantomime was gradually becoming obsolete was a discouraging thought...I had thought of possible voices for the tramp—whether he should speak in monosyllables or just mumble. But it was no use. If I talked I would become like any other comedian. These were the melancholy problems that confronted me.

Hal Roach: The greatest comedies that were made by anybody were made in two reels, I don't care who it was. It's a damn simple thing. If you can stop after 20 minutes, you've only got to up to this peak for your last laugh. But if you've got to go clear to 60 minutes, the last laugh is three times harder. It's that simple. And I don't care how funny a guy is, if you listen to him long enough, you're going to be bored to hell with him.

W.C. Fields: The work I'm doing on the screen differs from that of anyone else. My comedy is of a peculiar nature. Naturally no writers have developed along the lines of my type of comedy and that is why I have differences with writers, supervisors and directors alike. I am misunderstood mostly by these departments but the customers and the critics seem to get my point O.K.

DICK CAVETT ON W.C. FIELDS:
I had gone alone to a W.C. Fields movie at the New Yorker theatre and laughed my head off. On my way home I sat on a bench just inside the park and thought about Fields, and how he was dead, and what a master he was, and how I would never meet him, and how he could never conceive of how great he was and what he meant to me and to all the other people who appreciate his genius, some of which remains with you in a sort of afterglow when the laughter has faded—and the tears began to well up. It had to do with this...this frustration that such people can never see what they are, just once, plain, and be forever satisfied.

ANDRE SENNWALD (*NY TIMES* REVIEW OF "IT'S A GIFT"):
With the one exception of Charlie Chaplin, there is nobody but Mr. Fields who could manage the episode with the blind and deaf man in the store so as to make it seem genuinely and inescapably funny instead of just a trifle revolting.

JAMES AGEE ON W.C. FIELDS:
He was the toughest and most warmly human of all screen comedians, and *It's A Gift* and *The Bank Dick*, fiendishly funny and incisive white-collar comedies, rank

high among the best comedies (and best films) ever made.

MAE WEST ON W.C. FIELDS:
I think that under the grotesque ruin of a clown Bill Fields was tragically aware of the wreck he had made of himself.

W.C. FIELDS ON MAE WEST:
A plumber's idea of Cleopatra.

BUSTER KEATON ON THE MARX BROTHERS:
It was an event when you can get all three of them on the set at the same time. The minute you started a picture with the Marx Brothers, you hired three assistant directors, one for each Marx Brother. You had two of them while you went out to look for the the third one and the first two would disappear.

WOODY ALLEN ON THE MARX BROTHERS:
Their wit is so wonderful. The surrealism, the nonsensity and the unexplainable, unmotivated craziness is so fantastic. And, of course, the guys were talented! Chico was talented, Harpo was extremely talented, and Groucho was the best of them all.

MARTIN SHORT ON THE MARX BROTHERS:
I loved Groucho, but I was obsessed with Harpo. He was insane! It was just madness. It was great.

ALEXANDER WOOLLCOTT ON HARPO MARX:
Surely there should be dancing in the streets when a great clown comic comes to town, and this man is a great clown....Harpo Marx, so styled, oddly enough, because he

plays the harp, says never a word from first to last, but when by merely leaning against one's brother one can seem richly and irresistibly amusing why should one speak?

IRVING BRECHER ON WRITING FOR MARX BROS.:
[Producer] Mervyn LeRoy asked me to write a Marx Brothers film, which I did, called *At The Circus*. And then I wrote a second one, *Go West*, and that was enough for me. 'Cause I'd written both of them by myself…nobody'd ever done that. And I paid the price—I wound up with a tic. And the depression of writing a film for the Marx Brothers, who were wonderful people and friends of mine, but left all the decision-making about 'is this script okay or not?' to Groucho.

KITTY CARLISLE HART ON THE MARX BROTHERS:
Working with the Marx Bros. was unlike anything I had been led to expect. They never played tricks on me, they were unfailing courteous, and Groucho paid me the compliment of asking my opinion about the jokes. He was a worrier of the three. He would read me a line deadpan and ask, "Is that funny?" When I'd shake my head he'd go away, only to come back with another deadpan reading. He did it over and over, till he finally came up with a good one and I burst out laughing.

PHYLLIS DILLER ON GROUCHO MARX:
You realize my cigarette holder is Groucho's cigar, and my hair is Harpo's fright wig. So the Marx Brothers, and Groucho particularly,

since he was the comedian of the group, have influenced me.

GEORGE BURNS ON GROUCHO:
I said [at a party]…'If you want to know who I think is the funniest comedian, I would have to say Charlie Chaplin.' And Groucho resented that. He said, 'Charlie Chaplin isn't the funniest comedian. I am. I'm funnier than Chaplin.' So I said, Well, then I must be funnier than Charlie Chaplin too, because I'm funnier than you." And to make matters worse, I said, 'And Chaplin did it without his brothers!' Oh, Christ! Then Groucho came out and said, "George Burns has got no talent." I finally called him—I knew he wasn't feeling well—and I said, "Groucho, I changed my mind. You're funnier than Chaplin."

LARRY FINE:
We rehearsed a short three weeks before we shot it, which no other people did, even in features. We didn't just take a script and shoot it. We went to the studio every day, went through the routines, and tried to improve it and improve it. And I think it paid off…They're still shown after forty years. That's a lot longer than a lot of marriages last around here.

LUCILLE BALL ON THE THREE STOOGES:
The only thing I learned from [working with] them was how to duck!

MARTIN SHORT ON THE THREE STOOGES:
I love the Three Stooges. I like Curly. He was nuts. I'd never seen that behavior. It

was so big. You couldn't not look at him. And great physical grace.

MOE HOWARD ON CURLY HOWARD:
If he forgot his lines, it was a temporary thing. I could tell, because his eyes would roll around a little and he'd fall to the floor and spin around like a top—or do a backward kick, or go on his back and move like a snake.

LARRY FINE ON CURLY HOWARD:
Personally, I thought Curly was the greatest because he was a natural comedian who had no formal training. Whatever he did, he made up on the spur of the moment.

ED WYNN ON LAUREL & HARDY:
I walked into the commissary in 1933 [in Hollywood] to make a picture for MGM and one of them jumped up and said "Here's the master." I looked at him as though he was nuts because I thought *they* were the greatest.

EDDIE CANTOR ON LAUREL & HARDY:
It is their seriousness that strikes me most forcibly. They play everything as it it might be *Macbeth* or *Hamlet*. That, to me, has always been a true sign of comic genius.

STAN LAUREL ON OLIVER HARDY:
So terribly funny. He can still make me laugh like crazy after all these years.

STEVE ALLEN ON LAUREL & HARDY:
From early childhood, I have considered Laurel & Hardy funnier than Chaplin.

Leo McCarey on Laurel & Hardy:
> It's amazing how much thought went into what on the surface looked like low-down stupidity...Laurel was one of those rare comics intelligent enough to invent his own gags. He was remarkably talented. Hardy wasn't . That was the key to the Laurel-Hardy association.

Ricky Gervais on Laurel & Hardy:
> Whatever you do, whatever you talk about...it has to have empathy. You have to make that connection, and they did it...I want to hug them, and I can't laugh at someone I don't like.

Lou Costello on Laurel & Hardy:
> They were the funniest comedy team in the world.

Dick van Dyke on Laurel & Hardy:
> I worshipped the ground they walked on.

George Stevens on Laurel & Hardy:
> I was very much influenced by Laurel & Hardy...I was a youngster when I worked with [them], in my formative years. The whole thing was formative—nobody knew that Laurel & Hardy were going to be comedy stars...
>
> ...The beauty of Laurel & Hardy shorts to me was their absolute deliberation, their great poise, their Alphonse and Gaston relationship with one another. The Laurel & Hardy concept moved over into other films considerably, with Cary Grant, Roz Russell, Irene Dunne doing the late take

and even the double take. That had come out of the personalities of Laurel & Hardy, and the people that worked with them.

MICHAEL RICHARDS ON LAUREL & HARDY:
I've always…been fascinated by characters who can charm, characters who can bring an audience into a scene—without even speaking. I used to watch Laurel & Hardy do that all the time.

Chapter 5
The Radio Specialists

Fred Allen: In the theater, the actor had uncertainty, broken promises, constant travel and a gypsy existence. In radio, if you were successful, there was an assured season of work. The show could not close if there was nobody in the balcony. There was no travel and the actor could enjoy a permanent home. There may have been other advantages but I didn't need to know them.

Bob Hope: Radio was a medium where, every week, more people would hear my jokes than had see my vaudeville act in ten years on the Gus Sun Time [vaudeville circuit].

George Burns: We were all tough on our writers. I think a lot of that came from fear. Most of us had become successful by writing our own material, and it was hard for us to trust our careers to other people.

Fred Allen: It would enable the listener to flex his imagination, and perhaps make him want to follow the experiences of the characters involved. This, if it worked, would insure the radio comedian a longer life.

Jerry Stiller on Eddie Cantor:

His energy, his bulging eyes, his jet-black hair seemed to burst out of his body…His feet and hands were moving vertically and horizontally like piston rods. He looked like a puppet that had been given life and wanted us all to wonder at it…

To call it a radio show was a misnomer. When Eddie came to a joke he'd roll his eyes, which meant to us to laugh. He nodded his head when a joke didn't go over, which meant laugh anyway. When the show ended, Eddie seemed exhausted, but he performed a few encores. He gave us a great show, a great evening.

George Burns on Jack Benny:

No one was better suited for radio than Jack. Radio consisted of sound and silence. That was it. And while the rest of us were trying to figure out ways of using sound, Jack was smart enough to figure out how to use the silence. No one ever got more out of nothing than he did.

Irving Brecher (writer) on Jack Benny:

I was crazy about him, as a person. I always thought his—his and Fred Allen's—were the best comedy shows ever, on radio.

Steve Allen on Fred Allen:

There are several things that earmarked Fred's humor as distinctive. One was his sheer playful love of words. He had a poet's regard for peculiarities of sound and expression and seemed never so happy as when he could roll off his tongue some glittering allegory, metaphor or simile. He was actually much more intrigued by this sort of thing than he was by the simple joke.

ALAN KING ON FRED ALLEN:
He was brilliant; he was, as they say, too good for the room. We don't have wits like Fred Allen anymore, that was another time and another place.

GEORGE BURNS ON FRED ALLEN:
Fred Allen played a sarcastic, bitter, sometimes morbid, miserable, dejected, unhappy, sad comedian named Fred Allen. He was perfect for the part. The thing I always noticed about Fred was that he just wasn't happy unless he wasn't happy...[He] was radio's most popular pessimist. He was the kind of person who would look for the dark cloud inside the silver lining.

...A lot of people warned Fred that his dry wit wouldn't work on radio, and they kept warning him for the whole seventeen years his shows were on the air.

DICK CAVETT ON FRED ALLEN:
I saw him coming out the *What's My Line?* studio one rainy night, and I marveled that people were asking for the *other* panelists' autographs...When he got to the corner two bums came staggering out from a doorway, and one of them said, "You're the greatest, Fred." He turned and, in an aside to me, said, "ah, my fan club is gathering." It was funny and bitter, and I remember thinking,

"Fred Allen said something and I'm the only one who heard it."

JACK PAAR ON FRED ALLEN:
I had always looked up to Allen for his brilliant wit and satire. During the war I had sent him jokes from the South Pacific and he had replied in kind letters offering advice and criticism. After the war I met him at a small gathering in New York. "Mr. Allen," I blurted out, "you've always been my god!" "What a shame," he rasped. "Five hundred churches in New York, and you're an atheist."

HERMAN WOUK ON FRED ALLEN:
He was a role model and still is. Fred was one of the most honorable men I've ever met. He was the best comic writer radio ever developed, and here we were handing him what must have seemed like mediocre material. I was twenty-one years old and making two hundred dollars a week, a remarkable salary for the Depression. Not once did he tell us our contribution wasn't good enough.

FRED ALLEN:
For seventeen years, thirty-nine weeks each year, we had written and performed a 60-minute program…The work involved in writing and assembling a weekly radio show began to seem like a recipe for a nervous breakdown. During the early years it was fun. At this point it was drudgery. I was reading nine newspapers a day looking for subject matter for jokes.

Chapter 5: The Radio Specialists

EDGAR BERGEN ON W.C. FIELDS:

> The most talented man I ever worked with anywhere. He could read a joke somebody wrote for him. He could write his own joke and deliver it masterfully. And he was a master of pantomime—which had no part in radio of course, except for the occasional benefit of our studio audience.

KURT VONNEGUT ON BOB & RAY:

> My collected works would fill Oliver Hardy's derby, whereas theirs would fill the Astrodome...[they] had such energy and such a following that they continued to create marvelous material for radio at a time when radio creatively was otherwise dead.

JONATHAN WINTERS ON BOB & RAY:

> When you ask which direction I really came from, I've got to say Bob & Ray...they are two of the brightest talents in the business for my money.

Chapter 6
The War Years and Beyond

Bud Abbott: Ours is a talking act...we bellow all the time. One might call it corn, but we like it.

Moe Howard on Lou Costello:
I always felt there was much of Curly—his mannerisms and high pitched voice—in Costello's act in feature films.

Carol Burnett on Abbott and Costello:
I really do love slapstick. I think it's an art. I happen to think that Abbott and Costello were past masters at it...I think that they're classic.

Jerry Seinfeld on Abbott & Costello:
They were a seminal influence in my life. They made me fall in love with the idea of being funny. I loved them more than anything.

Ben Stiller on Abbott & Costello:
I grew up watching Abbott & Costello...I was into all of their films. I was getting them the second time around, but to me that was a big, influence.

BUSTER KEATON ON ABBOTT & COSTELLO:
> They'd say 'when do we come [to the movie set] and what do we wear?' Then they'd find out the day they'd start to shoot the picture what the script's about. Didn't worry about it, didn't try to. Well that used to get my goat because, my God, when we made pictures we ate, slept, and *dreamed* them.

WOODY ALLEN ON BOB HOPE:
> There was a time when he was still appearing in films where he was quite wonderful. The films are not always so wonderful...but he's always a very funny man in them. There are a number of films where he's allowed to show his brilliant gift of delivery, his brilliant gift of comic speech.

PAUL MAZURSKI ON DANNY KAYE:
> While he was a great performer, he wasn't really very funny. He was amusing. He was talented. But not deeply funny, not ironic... Sid Caesar was funny; Jackie Gleason was funny. Jack Benny was very funny. Danny Kaye was endearing, delightful, entertaining, tasteful, but he wasn't really funny.

ORSON WELLES ON JERRY LEWIS:
> When he goes too far, he's heaven; it's just when he doesn't go too far that he's unendurable. Now he wants to be a respected member of the community, and it shows in every move of his body. But God, he can be funny!

STEVE MARTIN ON JERRY LEWIS:
> I think he's a great comic. He sort of got a

bum rap. He's a very innovative and funny person, but because it's so silly and stupid, he's dismissed a lot. But silly and stupid has a big place in our lives.

MARTIN SHORT ON JERRY LEWIS: He's just a complicated guy. His personality can be hard to take. But when he became a star, it wasn't because people were interested in his personality. People weren't necessarily interested in the real Charlie Chaplin, either.

WOODY ALLEN ON JERRY LEWIS: Lewis is one of the most gifted and natural comic talents we've ever had. I've laughed hysterically at many of his films. I've seen him live and loved him.

JIM CARREY ON JERRY LEWIS: I love Jerry Lewis. I think he did some of the most astounding filmic clowning of anybody in history.

GROUCHO MARX ON JERRY LEWIS: Jerry Lewis hasn't made me laugh since he left Dean Martin.

PETER SELLERS: To see me as a person on the screen would be one of the dullest experiences you could ever wish to experience. But as soon as I can get a hold of something—a character or a voice or some make-up or something, I can then use that as a shield, get within it, and hope to make the character live—act as a medium, if you like—and let the character come out through me.

PETER SELLERS: Blake [Edwards] and I are like Laurel & Hardy together, we work out each gag to the tiniest detail, and still ad-lib a lot when the cameras are turning.

BLAKE EDWARDS ON PETER SELLERS:
There is an enormous love-hate relationship that goes on. It's a big strain at times, but he end result always seems to justify the anguish.

JERRY LEWIS ON JIM CARREY:
Jim Carrey is probably the best exponent of moving his body, and all of the attributes, of anyone that's been in the business for a hundred years. I've never seen anyone with a sense of time for the physical element to work, as opposed to a great monologist like Benny, who had a different time.

DICK VAN DYKE ON JIM CARREY:
Jim is a brilliant physical comedian. I mean, he's a class mime. He's the best I've ever seen.

JIM CARREY: A lot of my stuff is dumb, there's smart stuff in there too. I've been dubbed responsible for the dumbing of America. It's not up to me to educate America. I'm trying to give them relief.

MEL BROOKS ON EVERYBODY:
I thought Chaplin was wonderful. Liked Laurel and Hardy even more. Keaton was the greatest master of physical comedy. Fields was a genius at skit construction. And Fred Allen show me new kinds of irony.

Mort Sahl on Everybody:

> [Some comedians] are very serious fellows. Jonathan Winters is serious. Milton Berle is terrific. He's a great champion, so is Bob Hope, and so is Red Skelton. I'm very reverent of Sid Caesar, and of Jackie Gleason. The young people aren't. The new comedians aren't...I believe they're trying to escape comparison.

Billy Crystal on Everybody:

> If you look at any of the movies that any of the funny people do—I have great respect for the Marx Bros. and W. C. Fields and of those guys, and to be the offspring of that, its just a big family tree, people who do stuff that's funny, so I have great respect for those who proceeded me.

The Directors Speak

Roscoe "Fatty" Arbuckle:

> The same plot can be one over and over again in the so-called features but the comedy without new gags is a failure. That's why most comedy directors, after a while in the business, go around talking to themselves instead of giving out interviews. It's a hard life.

Stanley Kramer (on directing *It's a Mad, Mad, Mad, Mad World*):

> I had made the calculated assumption that, in a comedy, too much is better than too little...Those clowns had given me several thousand laughs off-screen, plus so many more onscreen, that I could be well-pleased by our accomplishment.

Steven Spielberg: I had always wanted to try a visual comedy… although there is nothing harder to accomplish than getting an audience to laugh. Getting an audience to scream at a shark or getting an audience to cry at the awesome wonders of outer space and some sort of extra-terrestrial rival is nothing compared to getting 800 people per screening to laugh out loud at something you think is funny. The sense of humor is so subjective and there is nothing more disappointing than expecting a laugh and not getting it—and nothing is more rewarding than getting the laughs where you hoped you would.

Mel Brooks: There's one thing you've got to understand before you can direct comedy. Comedy is serious—deadly serious. Never, never try to be funny. The actors must be serious. Only the situation must be absurd. Funny is in the writing, not in the performing. If the situation isn't absurd, no amount of hoke will help. And another thing, the more serious the situation, the funnier the comedy can be. The greatest comedy plays against the greatest tragedy.

Garry Marshall: As a director one of my aims with almost every picture is to walk the line between comedy and tragedy…Sometimes I walked it very well, sometimes the audience and I walked it well together. The critics don't always get it but I have always tried to combine it and not go too far. Sometimes I go too far and I immediately know it from the audience's reaction.

Chapter 7
The Television Legends

S.J. Perelman: It's not surprising that people who do weekly comedy shows on television are reduced to drivel.

David Steinberg: There is nothing as fleeting as a moment of wit on television.

Sid Caesar: When we did it, there were no cue cards, no teleprompters. It was live, live, live.

Milton Berle: It was murder. It was a rat race...In those early TV days, it was very, very difficult getting new material every week. For the first year I was on, '48 and '49, I didn't even have a writer. I just remembered what I did for the last twenty years, cause we couldn't afford a writer.

Jerry Lewis on Milton Berle:
The master. Without question. Berle was a very, very influential character.

Sid Caesar on Milton Berle:
Berle started it all. He is Mr. Television.

Dick Martin on Milton Berle:
When Milton Berle had his own show, he appeared in every sketch, while we're on ten

minutes every show. There aren't many comedians who could accept that. They think their shows can't survive without them on the screen constantly.

JACKIE GLEASON ON MILTON BERLE:
[If it] wasn't for Berle, a lot of us wouldn't have got a break either. When he became Mr. Television, those network guys began saying: 'We gotta get comics. They want funny stuff. Let's get funnymen.' Whatever else you say about Berle, don't forget that.

MILTON BERLE ON JACKIE GLEASON:
When Gleason does *The Honeymooners*, which is one of the great masterpieces of all times...even though there is a lot of Gleason in it, he won't step down out of character to speak to the audience. He will not break up the sketch or the scene to do an ad-lib.

ART CARNEY ON JACKIE GLEASON:
He was the only star I ever worked with who said, 'go for more.' If you got a big laugh, that was fine. If you got two laughs, that was better. He didn't worry about me upstaging him or showing him up—although when it came to being spontaneously funny, he was pretty damn fast on his feet.

SID CAESAR:
We never used cue cards [on *Your Show of Shows*] and I'll tell you why not. Acting is through the eyes. If you're looking at someone, you can see what they're doing. You can feel what they're doing. If you're looking off at cue cards, you lose that connection.

BILLY CRYSTAL ON SID CAESAR:

> The first thing that I know that I saw on television that made me laugh was Sid Caesar playing Yul Brynner in *The King And I*...I was a little kid, and I still remember the bit.

CONAN O'BRIEN ON SID CAESAR:

> I was very influenced early on by Sid Caesar. He did a "This Is Your Life" sketch. [His character] panics, he doesn't want to be on TV. He starts to run...Sid Caesar wasn't winking and letting everyone know it was a sketch. He desperately was this guy who didn't want to be on "This Is Your Life," so he's trying to run away. He really committed to it, and that's what made it so funny. And that's what I loved. And I was laughing and tears were coming down my face. And I knew that's what I wanted to do.

TERRY GILLIAM ON SID CAESAR:

> I remember...watching Sid Caesar's *Your Show of Shows*. It was brilliant.

RICHARD PRYOR ON SID CAESAR:

> I was intimidated meeting Caesar and also having to keep up with his quick mind. "I can do German," he said. "What about you?" I stared at him and said to myself, "Goddam, Sid Caesar's talking to me."

LARRY GELBART ON SID CAESAR:

> Sid was a very good judge of material. All really good comedians are very good editors. They recognize what's right for them, they definitely know what's wrong

for them. And he was brave. We would do satires or parodies based on material that was not generally well known or widespread. We did very esoteric things and brave things, and Sid was the bravest of all because he was the one out there in front of the camera doing it and risking his reputation and his ability to make people laugh by doing material that was very sophisticated.

WOODY ALLEN ON SID CAESAR:
Writing for Caesar was the highest thing you could aspire to—at least as a TV comedy writer. The Presidency was above that.

MEL BROOKS ON SID CAESAR:
Charlie Chaplin could not have done what Sid Caesar did. No living human being could have done that amount of great comedy for so long a period—live, an hour and a half for nine years on television. It's impossible, but Sid Caesar carried us all on his big, broad shoulders…He raised the level of comedy in America many, many notches.

JOHN LITHGOW ON SID CAESAR:
I remember Sid Caesar as this sort of great comic genius. We loved his crazy German patter, we loved his Tramp, his partnership with Imogene Coca, he was kind of like the gravitational center of this crazy wonderful ensemble.

TRACEY ULLMAN ON IMOGENE COCA:
Imogene Coca was fantastic. And it wasn't that forced kind of comedy, or she wasn't

having to be—I keep coming back to this, but it was very true in my childhood that women had to be sexy to be comedians, it seemed, or to be on TV—and she was just very endearing, and her timing was superb.

LILY TOMLIN ON IMOGENE COCA:
Imogene Coca would do characters and different accents on Your Show of Shows. I was so attracted to her comic striptease routine that I copied it—stole it!—when I was in college.

LARRY GELBART ON MEL BROOKS:
Being present at the birth of countless comic miracles that this totally unique talent is capable of creating, being surprised and blindsided on a daily basis by his extraordinary and completely unique take on humor, I became convinced that no one could be Mel Brook's kind of funny without some sort of divine assistance.

BILLY CRYSTAL ON MEL BROOKS:
To me, he's the funniest man in the world.

CARL REINER ON MEL BROOKS:
Mel Brooks to me is the funniest human being I know.

WOODY ALLEN:
Everything I learned about comedy writing I learned from Danny Simon. He turned my professional career around completely.

CAROL BURNETT ON JACK BENNY:
When somebody would say something that would get a laugh, Jack would pause, and the audience would start to laugh, and he

had the courage to keep pausing, to not try to fill that silence, because the more he would drag it out, the funnier it became until it was sidesplitting.

JERRY SEINFELD ON JACK BENNY:
Comedy strength is slowness. Jack Benny is a perfect example. He would come onstage and not say anything. He would just stand there and people would start to laugh. I mean, that is comic strength.

GROUCHO MARX ON JACK BENNY:
He was a great comedian and one of the nicest men I ever knew.

BOB NEWHART ON JACK BENNY:
I've always said that he was the bravest comic that I've ever seen work because he wasn't afraid of silence. That's something you have to learn. You have to take the time to tell it right and not rush it. Not think, 'Oh my God, they're not laughing.' Jack was a master of that. His timing was incredible.

STAN LAUREL ON JACK BENNY:
A real craftsman. He knows what consistent comedy characterization is. The only criticism I have to offer is that once in a while he holds after his laughs too long. He milks those "holds" on occasion and he shouldn't.

ALBERT BROOKS ON JACK BENNY:
Jack was the greatest there ever was at doing nothing. He could bring the house down by staring off into space.

STEVE MARTIN ON JACK BENNY:
...[He] couldn't exist today because when he took the pause somebody would yell out something, which would ruin everything.

PHIL SILVERS ON JACK BENNY:
It must be a little dull to be Jack Benny for one reason. I don't know anybody who doesn't love him.

LUCILLE BALL: To my delight, I discovered that the *I Love Lucy* show drew from everything I'd learned in the movies, radio, the theatre, and vaudeville. I wanted everything about the venture to be top-flight: the timing, the handling of props, the dialogue. We argued a good deal at first because we all cared so passionately; sometimes we'd discuss phrasing or word emphasis in a line of dialogue until past midnight.

FRAN DRESCHER ON LUCILLE BALL:
I loved '*I Love Lucy.*' She was beautiful but also very comedic and physical with her comedy and I thought, that's the way to be if you're going to star in your own television show. The thing that I think is most noteworthy is that she drove the story, yet she was also the clown.

STAN LAUREL ON RED SKELTON:
I love his talent but I hate the thing he does with it when he does that deliberate and undeliberate breaking up. In my opinion this is the worst possible thing any comedian can do—the worst. And he even lets some of his untalented guests do it. Dreadful.

Red Skelton: People say to me, why do you laugh at your own jokes? Well, I figure, why, if I have five thousand people sitting in the audience, why should I be the only guy not getting the joke?

Lucille Ball on Red Skelton: I always thought Red, one of the world's great talents, is basically a very sad clown…In his most outlandish buffoonery, he makes me cry more than he makes me laugh. Something about him is just inescapably poignant.

Marcel Marceau on Red Skelton: In his field he had no peer; he was unique in his way of clowning. He was elite and at the same time so humble. He was a master of telling stories and jokes, and a great human soul.

Groucho Marx on Red Skelton: I think the logical successor to Chaplin is Skelton. Red, to my mind, is the most unacclaimed clown in show business…He also sings, dances, delivers a deceptively simple comic monologue and plays a dramatic scene about as effectively as any of the dramatic actors, Method or otherwise.

George Wallace on Red Skelton: I just think he was the best. He's the reason I'm in this business. I loved him doing the characters, everything he could do just cracked me up. I just loved him.

Red Skelton: I just want to be known as a clown because to me that's the height of my profession. It means you can do everything—sing, dance, and above all, make people laugh.

TOM SMOTHERS ON GEORGE GOBEL:
I always wanted to be a comedian. When I first saw George Gobel, who was my first influence, I was 12 or 13...He was on the Ed Sullivan Show. I thought it was marvelous what this man did. I told my principal, "that's what I'd like to do."

CHEVY CHASE ON ERNIE KOVACS:
Ernie Kovacs was a video innovator. He knew that there was an intrinsic magic about television itself that should be explored...He could do a 'sketch' in a restaurant setting as well as the next man. What is memorable about Ernie was his inclination to stay away from the familiar. He chose to break precedents whenever possible.

TERRY GILLIAM ON ERNIE KOVACS:
He was a surrealist and I'd never really come across surrealism before, so it was the funniest thing I'd ever seen. It freed me, because up to that point everything had been so literal and suddenly there were these incredible leaps showing that a thing didn't have to be what it was.

DAN ROWAN ON ERNIE KOVACS:
Ernie was definitely way ahead of his time...[He] did recognize the visual possibilities of television and I would say that, if he were alive, he probably would have done our kind of show long before we ever did.

STEVE MARTIN ON STEVE ALLEN:
He brought a gaiety to comedy. He defined the term "off-the-wall" in the late '50s and early '60s.

DAVID LETTERMAN ON STEVE ALLEN:
He had a great mind for stuff to do on television. We said, 'Well, heck, let's just steal off of those great ideas.'

STEVE ALLEN:
You have to control yourself to the point where you never become smart-alecky or superior. If I had been rude or cruel, the laughter would have stopped immediately.

CAROL BURNETT ON DICK VAN DYKE:
Dick van Dyke would have been a star in silent films because of his body, his movements. He's a naturally funny clown.

TED DANSON ON DICK VAN DYKE:
He was very graceful, very fluid, and he did make it look effortless. But I think when things look effortless, it's usually because somebody's rehearsed, rehearsed, rehearsed...As a physical comedian, I love how he used his body to be funny or to express some character thing, and I think Dick van Dyke in a comedic form is about as good as it gets.

DICK VAN DYKE ON CARL REINER:
I think I learned the most working with Carl Reiner than I ever did...about comedy, about human behavior, about everything.

JERRY SEINFELD ON CARL REINER:
I think Carl Reiner is funnier than Mark

Twain. Twain would be lucky to be typing script changes for Carl Reiner.

DICK CAVETT ON JERRY LEWIS:
Jerry had been hilarious [on TV] because he was a guest. It may be funny to see a man tear up someone else's place, but it is embarrassing to see him tear up his own. It was bizarre and funny to see Jerry go on Ed Sullivan's show, push Ed into the wings, and pull the TelePrompTer apart and rip the paper out of it. But when he did that kind of thing on his own show it wasn't funny so much as it was puzzling...Still, Jerry is a huge raw talent. Someday he may surrender himself totally to a genius director, and the result could be a masterpiece.

TED DANSON ON EVERYBODY:
I wish I had grown up with a television because I so honor those that have come before me—Sid Caesar, Mel Brooks, Lucille Ball was obviously amazing—that whole group, they were like pioneers, they started comedy in television.

STEVE ALLEN ON LILY TOMLIN:
She is unquestionably one of our greatest comediennes. She is, however, by no means always the funniest.

TRACEY ULLMAN ON LILY TOMLIN:
She's just so versatile and smart...it's the sadness of the people she impersonates that makes them funny was well.

RICHARD PRYOR ON LILY TOMLIN:
She turned me on. I went gaga over the way

she dressed up in various outfits and became all those different people. I thought she was phenomenal and loved watching her work. She'd make me goofus from laughing so hard. Then she'd switch gears and inject a poignancy that made you think about the way you looked at the world. That was inspiring. It took comedy to a different level.

If not for her, I never would've gotten anywhere.

FLIP WILSON: I was doing preacher stories and the Geraldine voice as the voice of females in the stories I told onstage. When I went to TV, I realized people relate to different characters. I wanted to make it like a fruit cocktail and bring those characters to life.

JAY LENO ON FLIP WILSON:
His sketches seemed much fresher than what anybody else was doing...It's so hard to be original and still have mass appeal. Flip was hip, but her made sure everybody could understand him and laugh. That's the sign of a great performer.

STEVE ALLEN ON FLIP WILSON:
Nobody ever sent him a postcard objecting to any of his humor. There was no vulgarity, there was no sleaze, there were no shock jokes. It was just funny. I wish we had more like him today.

MILTON BERLE ON FLIP WILSON:
Flip Wilson was an incredible performer,

one of the funniest people I ever knew...a comedy genius.

THE SKETCH COMEDIANS

SID CAESAR: The sketch is a lost art. With a sketch all you need is a table and chairs. You can do the same thing in a 10-minute sketch that you do in a two-hour movie—but without the padding.

JERRY LEWIS ON GLEASON: The best sketch comedian I'd ever seen in my life.

TIM CONWAY: I've never tried to be number one, I'm more comfortable as a second banana.

HARVEY KORMAN ON TIM CONWAY: He's a second banana genius. So what, so he's not a "star." He is in my eyes.

CAROL BURNETT ON TIM CONWAY: There's a genius. I have seen him take four-page sketches and turn them into 25 minutes of one, long howl from the audience. It has nothing to do with the writing. It's Tim.

CHEVY CHASE ON JOHN BELUSHI: I worked with him years before *Saturday Night Live*. He was very good physically. He was very funny sometimes. He wasn't so great other times. He wasn't any better or worse than myself or Danny [Aykroyd] or Billy [Murray] on any given occasion. He had a certain style—a boring-in, gruff attitude that was displayed well in *Animal House*. He was also a fairly insecure, not highly well-read, short, heavy fellow who needed friends.

TRACEY ULLMAN ON GILDA RADNER:
Gilda Radner especially in the 70s was a big inspiration of mine. She's really likable. All of her characters were funny and yet they had a likable quality. She was very physically appealing, the way she moved around, and her energy, and she has a very likable, open face.

MARTIN SHORT: I do a particular kind of comedy. It's sketch oriented, character oriented. Not many jokes. If you were to read a script that I've written, there's not many jokes in it. You just have to trust me. Some people like it and some people don't I really do feel like I'm a little boxer struggling out my own particular point of view. And that's very rewarding, because it's specific.

BENNY HILL: My ideal form of entertainment is to have it all going on at once: good music, pretty girls, lots of laughs. I sometimes use a girl singer the way Henny Youngman uses his violin as a bridge between one laugh and the next."

THE LATE-NIGHT HOSTS

BILL COSBY ON JACK PAAR:
If you got on the Jack Paar Show, if you performed well, it opened up all of the nightclubs for you to play. So when Jack

Paar put the stamp on you, that was it for you. You could name your booking.

DAVID LETTERMAN ON JACK PAAR:
I've always been a big fan of Jack Paar's. I had met him, and he had invited me to his home a couple of times. I had always found him to be really interesting and still very energetic and dynamic, and I had wanted to get him on the show. But the response was that he had been advised by friends not to go on our show because we would make fun of him. I was saddened by that.

HENNY YOUNGMAN ON JOHNNY CARSON:
I think Carson is great, I think he's the best. He lets you do your thing even if he knows the joke. He lets comedians work, he encourages you, he laughs at you. He enjoys what you do.

GARRY SHANDLING ON JOHNNY CARSON:
I was enormously influenced by Carson. In fact, if I had any early comedic goal, it was to be a stand-up comedian and do the *Tonight Show*. He is funnier than anyone knows. If you watch the show even on what he would call his off nights, there was still wit about him.

DAVID LETTERMAN ON JOHNNY CARSON:
I don't even watch the *Tonight Show* because how good he is makes me nervous and insecure. I look at that show, and I say to myself, "Yeah, see, you're no Johnny Carson.

DON RICKLES ON JOHNNY CARSON:
Carson had a great secret—he left spaces

that made you always look good. I never came off that show where I didn't say, 'God, I was so good," because of him. And he was a funny, funny man. Still is.

JOAN RIVERS ON JOHNNY CARSON: As a stand-up comedian, Johnny had an easy, WASPy charm. He came up as a boyish MC, and he never seemed to want to develop any great routines. You never thought, Jesus Christ, that was funny—like Woody Allen's moose routine, George Carlin doing the Seven Words You Can't Say, or Bill Cosby doing Noah. But Carson is still one of the great straight men of the century. He is a brilliant reactor who becomes the audience, asking its questions, having its reactions. This is extremely difficult.

GARRY SHANDLING: I was mesmerized by comedians I saw on *The Tonight Show*. That was really how I saw and learned about comedians, like Don Rickles, Steve Allen, and George Carlin.

CONAN O'BRIEN: I remember watching Letterman once and getting this feeling while I was watching him, like, Yeah, what he's doing, I could do that. Or watching Johnny and thinking, Maybe that's it.

I'm a very specific person. I didn't want to be a stand-up comic. Not because I don't like stand-up, but because my skill is sitting down, playing with ideas, interacting with people and maybe getting something funny out of them. I was an improvisational performer for years, which helped me learn how to listen. When you're on the air, you can't be thinking about what joke you're gong to make next. You just have to shut up and listen and wait until they say something you can play off of.

JON STEWART: News used to hold itself to a higher plane and slowly it as dissolved into, well, me...The main thing I don't want to be is unfunny. That's really the mandate. Just whatever we're doing, make it as funny as we can possibly make it.

Chapter 8
The Stand-Up Comedians

Garry Marshall: You can call a comic many things but never a coward...Night after night, comics get up onstage all alone with just a microphone and take a chance, knowing that if a line misses, a comic faces a mean wave of silence with his mouth drying, brow sweating, and legs shaking. There is no way out...I know because I've been there. It's terrifying. That's why the first stand-up comedians were court jesters who usually were deformed: Nobody else wanted the job.

What Does It Take?

Ray Romano: To do stand-up, to be a comedian, to know what's funny, even though it seems very simple, actually you need to have some type of intelligence. It's not book smart, that's for sure. But you need to have insight and a little bit of perception, to know, even though comedy looks as simple as it does, there's probably a lot more that goes into it.

Richard Lewis: It's got to make me laugh first, because if it does, that's what gives me the courage to go out there and share it with strangers. And if something sounds hilarious to the masses but doesn't amuse me at all, there's no way I would ever say it.

Jerry Seinfeld: There are two kinds of conviction—because even if you don't believe 100 per cent in the idea behind the joke, you've got to believe 100 percent that it's funny. There has to be conviction somewhere.

Phil Foster: Look at people and pick up on their mistakes and inadequacies. Watch human behavior. Telling the truth about people will make them laugh.

Jay Leno: People look at musicians and think, 'Now that's something not everyone can do,' but because everyone can talk and be funny (to some degree), a comic doesn't get the same respect as a guitar player or even a guy who's banging garbage can lids on the street.

Bob Newhart: Comedians can only discuss certain things with other comedians because if you have never done stand-up, you don't know what it's like. You don't know the feel of an audience.

Woody Allen: The best material in the world in the hands of a hack or someone who doesn't know how to deliver jokes is not going to mean anything. You can take the worst material in the world and give it to W.C. Fields or Groucho Marx and something funny will come out.

Carol Leifer: I kind of have lofty ideas for comedy—that it should be life-affirming and make you feel good; in that respect, I'm a big fan of Jay Leno and Jerry Seinfeld.

BILLY CRYSTAL: I've been a stand-up comic for a long time, and a good one. But a stand-up is different things to different people. To me, it's a man or a woman who goes out in front of people emotionally naked and talks about real things.

JERRY SEINFELD: Stand-up is real. No matter how famous you are, if you're not funny, they're not laughing. Laughter is an involuntary response. People don't laugh just because you're successful.

BRETT BUTLER: There are a few kids out there right now raking in cash for rapidly taking toys out of a trunk, saying something funny about it, and then doing the same thing all over again. Who am I to say that's any less artistic than stand-ups who talk about airplanes and old people driving?

DAVID LETTERMAN: I don't think I was a good stand-up comedian. I could do the job. I learned the skills of making a roomful of drunks laugh. But I never really enjoyed it. I always felt like I was not enough. To me, when you go see a comic, you want to see a guy like Gallagher. You want to see lights and props and balloons and fruit being smashed. You want to see something because you're spending something like 20 to 25 bucks. They came to see me, and all I really had was 30 minutes of jokes.

Writing Jokes

RAY ROMANO: Some bits take a long time [to develop]. I've had bits in my act that literally—a year and a half later I'm still developing them and honing them. "I found the exact right way to say it last night," you know…so you're writing onstage.

RITA RUDNER: Every day I went to the library and got as many books and records about comedy as I could. I would go to the Museum of Broadcasting and look at old shows. I did my own little comedy course. I studied every day. I worked for months on that first five minutes of material. A lot of people approached comedy as a lark. Not me.

BOB NEWHART: Especially in a new piece of material, you write what I call exit doors. You write to a certain spot where you can get out, in case it isn't working. Then you write to another exit door, and you get out there if it isn't working. And you just keep going from one exit door [to the next], and before you know it, you've got six minutes.

LARRY MILLER: I analyze down to commas—and I love it. Comics are like poets. No one would ever think to say to a poet, 'Gee, why did you have to add that extra syllable to a line?' That's what poetry is all about—a thousand different considerations—balance, rhythm, texture. And so is comedy.

BUDDY HACKETT: First I hear a punchline, I hear something funny. And then I build a story on the front of it.

HENNY YOUNGMAN: To me, the key is to keep the joke compact. You want to make it easy for the audience to *visualize* the gag.

CHRIS ROCK: You got to write. Just got to find your own voice and study. You got to really be on top of what everybody's doing and what everybody did before you.

RODNEY DANGERFIELD: If you can't write your own material, you have very little chance of making it as a comedian. When you're starting out, just try to get five minutes of good material, then work on it and work on it until you think it's great.

HENNY YOUNGMAN: It still bothers some people when the learn that some of their favorite comics don't write all of their own material. But what can you do? It's show business...Still, I cannot tell you how happy I am that I came up with my own signature joke, "Take my wife, please!" It just wouldn't seem right to have purchased your signature joke, if you know what I mean.

JACKIE MASON: There's nothing wrong with doing words that somebody else wrote, if you can do them effectively and get the same laugh. Who says you have to write it yourself? But I don't find that I need somebody else to write for me. I like what I come up with, and I'm involved in my own thoughts, and it expresses my own ideas. One of the pleasures in my mind as much as performing it is the thought of it. And I like to be the one who thought of it.

MILTON BERLE: Walter Winchell labeled me "The Thief of Bad Gags." The image of a joke stealer is fine with me. I've capitalized on it…the same way that Jack Benny has built on his being cheap. It's when somebody in the business takes it seriously—and they should know better—that it hurts.

WORKING ONSTAGE

GARRY SHANDLING: I still enjoy walking into a club and getting up onstage. I think I'm still growing as a comedian. There's no better feeling creatively than coming up with new material, performing it the same day, and getting an immediate response. That's a cliche, but it's true. It's so in the moment.

JERRY SEINFELD: I adjust my act every night in front of every audience. In fact, I can tell what type of people they are and what their sense of humor is. That said, though, I don't think 'Here's something that people will like.' I start with what I like.

BILL DANA: It's the old physical law of equal reaction to every action—if you dig the audience, they dig you back. If you don't like them, boy, that's exactly what you get back in equal proportion.

RODNEY DANGERFIELD: From the moment you walk onstage, try to make the people like you. That's the most important thing. If they like you, you can get a big laugh with a mediocre joke. If they don't like you, you've got some serious thinking to do about your career choice.

BOB NEWHART: Stand-up comedy is not for the faint of heart or small of ego...If the audience doesn't laugh, they're saying, "You're not funny." And that's personal.

DAVID BRENNER: If I'm just very funny, it doesn't matter because the audience *expects* me to be funny. I gotta do something where they'll say, 'Oh, my God, no one else had the guts to do that.'

JACK BENNY: I'll tell you what timing is. Timing is not so much knowing when to speak, but when to pause. Timing is pauses.

JOAN RIVERS: Comedy is half music. So much has to do with rhythms and timing—when a beat comes, when a rest comes. If somebody sets you up wrong, it's like a conductor tapping his baton; you have to reset yourself, and start again.

HENNY YOUNGMAN: To be honest, I've never understood all this technical talk of stuff like comic 'timing.' When masters like Groucho Marx told me to slow down in my delivery to milk the audience and save material, I refused to pay heed. Who's got time, I figured, for proper transitions and segues between jokes?

CAROL LEIFER: Joke telling is a dying art form. You know, "Two guys walk into a bar..." that kind of thing. That part of comedy intrigues me. It's sad to me that it's really kind of dying out.

CHRIS ROCK: People are paying twenty-five bucks, they want a performance. They don't want me, they want me to be better than me. I gotta look *better* than me, be taller, louder, I have to be *more*.

RITA RUDNER: I'm not a hard-hitting comedian, and I never like to use a rhythm or a voice that says, 'the punch line is coming now.' I kind of like to have people say, 'oh, that was the punch line.' It's the way I talk in real life. It's natural. It's the style that evolved and that I was comfortable with.

JAY LENO: I was once asked why I was afraid to tick off my audience. They're my audience! Why would I want to tick them off? I just don't understand the logic there. To me, if you're a comedian, you should make everybody laugh. Everybody. Case closed.

DICK SMOTHERS: We exaggerate our natural tendencies when we get into comedy, and then it's believable. If you create somebody who's not there, I think you have to be a superior actor to let anybody buy it. I'm pretty logical. Basically, if things don't make any sense to me, I don't want to do it. And that's the way I control our relationship onstage with Tommy. He would go off on a tangent and I would correct him."

JAY LENO: There are two kinds of comedians. There are comedians that have a lot of attitude and not many jokes, there are are comedians that have a lot of jokes but not much stage persona. To me the best comedians are the kind that combine both of those elements—you have a joke and you have an attitude.

Andrew Dice Clay: I know the difference between the person and the performer. On stage, I am not the boy next door, but off stage, I am. And what people should realize is that it's a joke.

Janeane Garofalo: I don't do joke-jokes per se. I have buzzwords written on this piece of paper in my notebook, or sometimes they're written on my hand…but I don't like to memorize whole bits because it feels like I'm regurgitating by rote.

Johnny Carson: Ad-libbing isn't very often the instant creation of a good line. More often it's remembering things you've used before and maybe making a quick switch to a fresh situation.

Carol Leifer: Whenever I think of advice, I can quote Jay [Leno] on a million things. But I think the best thing he ever said to me was, 'Don't ever remind the audience that you only work twenty minutes a day. They probably worked eight hours, came out to a how, they're tired and the last thing they want to hear is how easy *your* job is.

Shades of Blue

David Brenner: The purpose of comedy is to make people laugh. I work clean; other comedians work totally blue. But funny is funny.

Lenny Bruce: Well, as far as working dirty is concerned, I had an influence there—Harry Truman.

Sinbad: I was on stage and I was dying. I didn't

really know how to do comedy and I was trying to write stuff rather than just be what I am. And I remember I cursed on stage. And it was one of the worst feelings I ever had. People were laughing, but I said I would quit comedy before I had to do that. It was like I was forced to do this to get laughter. People would laugh, but I'm going, 'But this is not funny. What I said before, I'm just cursing. I had said four or five bad words. I'll never do that again…I believe anybody who uses profanity can be clean and funny.

BILLY CRYSTAL: I have one of the grossest minds around… It's just not what I choose to give an audience.

PAUL RODRIGUEZ: I believe that the only offensive joke is a joke that's not funny.

FLOP SWEAT

BOB NEWHART: If you get enough comedians together, they'll eventually wind up talking about the time they died onstage.

BRETT BUTLER: The sound of silence during what was supposed to be a comedy routine is louder than one might think.

JAY LENO: Some people just won't laugh at a joke for whatever reason. You just have to keep going. But sometimes it's even funnier if a joke flops—people like to see you squirm. They'll laugh at that, and you just have to take it with a grain of salt. You can't get offended.

Chris Rock: I've definitely been booed off the stage, a couple of times. You know the old saying, 'Just get back on a horse,' you know? It's my fault. It's always my fault...I always blame me. I don't care if I'm playing a prison and half the audience is deaf or whatever, if I don't get laughs, it's my fault. So I rethought the act and came back right and didn't get booed.

Margaret Cho: Most of the time it would go fine, and people would laugh and I'd stand a little taller and feel a little more confident. Sometimes, I wasn't very good. Time would drag and I'd leave the stage defeated, but it never felt as bad as I thought it would. Afterward, I would try to get back on stage as soon as possible, to erase what I had done, to get some kind of performance retribution.

Don Rickles: I always say in comedy...there's always somebody, when you stand alone and you're selling yourself, doesn't particularly care for you...when you sell yourself you can't please everybody. But when you're different, you can last. And I've been very lucky, because I've been different. And I had some tough times in my beginnings, but thank God, that's what carried me through, to still get a job and people still show up.

Mort Sahl: You'll notice that a lot of the rules that comedians come up with are really rationalizations for failure, reasons why the audience doesn't laugh at them. If you said that talent was an absolute, they wouldn't be interested in enforcing that rule. The whole thing an artist has to do is create a reality and absorb the audience into it. And the good guys can do that, while the no-talents can't. It's as simple as that.

THE GREEN-EYED MONSTER

JACKIE MASON: I'm not too close to too many comedians. I find that there's too much jealousy among comedians. This is a very, very insecure and nerve-wracking business.

MILTON BERLE: When I started to hit it big, the hate started pouring out of the other comedians. They didn't seem to mind me on the way up, but when I started to arrive, they suddenly didn't like me. I got hate letters from Ed Wynn, Eddie Cantor, Lou Holtz, Al Jolson, and many other biggies, accusing me of stealing from them.

BILLY CRYSTAL: Jealousy is a terrible emotion because you create your own. It's very, very destructive. Eats people up. Jealousy is the crack of comics.

RICHARD PRYOR: Bill Cosby was the guy who was most envied. I remember seeing a picture of Bill on the cover of *Time* magazine. Every comedian I knew had seen it and was ealous as an ugly whore. But damn, Bill was good.

BILLY CRYSTAL: I was jealous of Freddy Prinze, because he made it big so suddenly. But I understood why. There's a difference between a star and a superstar—a look in the eye. A little something that's off, and Freddy had that. When he went on stage, it was *boom!*

The Wannabes

Phyllis Diller: All new comics can learn from their peers, and the people who came before, because you don't go to college to study comedy.

Richard Belzer: People who have a vague idea of what it's like to put a joke together are going up and making a living....I don't begrudge anyone trying to do stand-up, I'm just a little distressed by how the industry's been diluted with such mass amounts of mediocre comics.

Is there anybody [today] who can compare to Jack Benny, or Lenny Bruce, or Jonathan Winters?

Jay Leno: The sad thing is I go to the clubs now and I meet a lot of comics who aren't doing the work. They're just up there screwing around, having fun. Their friends come in and sit in the first couple of rows, yell obscenities back and forth. Then they sort of do bits and step off the stage...Then you go out on the road where people don't know you and obviously they're not going to pay you the same money. So,[the comics] 'cop an attitude' and go back to wherever they're from and never get a chance to grow, or do anything different. They get stuck in the same endless thing all the time.

Jerry Lewis: Anyone who does comedy well makes me laugh. I'm a pushover. I love it. The sadness for me is when I see someone that shouldn't be doing comedy that's doing it—cerebral combat—the kid who walks out in a comedy club and dares the audience to understand what the hell he's talking about.

Richard Belzer: There was a guy [I saw] onstage doing a Lenny Bruce routine. I was just aghast and shocked. He was just stealing his material. And I heard these two guys in back of me, and one says, "hey, that's my Lenny Bruce bit." Third generation stolen material.

Brett Butler: My favorite [comedy club] shows were ones when I worked with other monologists. In the end, though, we were all trying to do the same thing—be the center of attention and get famous for it.

The Borscht Belt/Nightclub Comics

Alan King on Martin & Lewis: I've been watching comedy for over fifty years. I guess I've seen every comedy act, big and small, in the world. And nobody did what Martin and Lewis did to an audience. I mean, people laughed so hard they turned over tables and knocked down chairs. I'm talking about delirium.

Jerry Lewis on Dean Martin: After the first night he was on stage with me, I knew we had lightning in a bottle.

BILL MAHER ON DEAN MARTIN:
> When the history of comedy is written by someone who really knows the subject, he or she will have to give Dean his rightful due...His timing was impeccable, and he had to be the smoothest straight man ever to play the game.

DICK VAN DYKE ON MOREY AMSTERDAM:
> He had a mental Rolodex of [jokes] and I could practically hear the shuffling as he searched for the right comeback.

GEORGE BURNS ON SHECKY GREENE:
> It's impossible not to laugh at Shecky Greene. He's so funny...and he's clever. He can say anything. He can dance and he can sing and he's wild and he can take falls, but he's basically funny. You see there are comedians who are very good but they are not funny...to me.

DON RICKLES ON JACK E. LEONARD:
> I know Jack claims I've been doing his act, but at least I've been trying to improve it.

BRAD GARRETT ON DON RICKLES:
> The first time I ever saw Don Rickles on *The Tonight Show* is when I knew I wanted to do stand up, because I couldn't believe this guy would come on and create this, and talk to these legends the way that he did and get away with it, and be funny.

CARL REINER ON BUDDY HACKETT:
> An extraordinarily creative and bright comedian who was as unpredictable and volatile as he was creative.

JERRY LEWIS ON HENNY YOUNGMAN:
> Shecky [Greene] does two hours on a stage, Norm [Crosby] can do the same, I can do the same, and we never ever do anything without set-ups, preparation, go for the joke, build it, and then, bang, get the laugh. Henny Youngman was fearless. He would say anything, as fast as he possibly could, to get out and get the money and to go to sleep.

MILTON BERLE ON HENNY YOUNGMAN:
> He gave me a couple of jokes, and I talked to him about timing, delivery, doing a monologue. I didn't go near his natural style of delivery, which was fast but easy. That was Henny from the beginning. He once said he was the King of the One-Liners, but I told him that was because he couldn't remember two.

RED BUTTONS ON HENNY YOUNGMAN:
> He had a knowing wit coupled with an original delivery...[He] was a kid at heart, a heart that belonged to a true clown, a far greater achievement than being a king.

JERRY STILLER ON HENNY YOUNGMAN:
> Henny was a magician: His trick was that he could make anyone laugh. His only prop was his wit. He was an intellect in the garb of a clown....He dared you not to laugh. More often than not you would and he lived to tell another joke.

STEVE ALLEN ON HENNY YOUNGMAN:
> His style is so traditional, so Borscht Belt that he could probably do Mort [Sahl]'s

whole act and it would still sound like Henny Youngman.

JOAN RIVERS ON TOTIE FIELDS:
Totie was a throwback to the tough, vulgar Catskill comics...She was a brilliant comic, singing a couple of songs, talking, doing routines about pantyhose, about her husband George, about being fat. She came out of the lowest levels of show business, from toilets, a fat girl doing strip joints. And she was a total professional who knew how to work an audience, how to sell a joke.

ALAN KING ON DANNY THOMAS:
Danny Thomas was probably the greatest influence on my show business life. When I saw Danny Thomas, I knew what I had to do.

THE 'NEW WAVE' COMEDIANS OF THE '50S

LENNY BRUCE ON SHELLEY BERMAN:
A brilliant satirist. But he's a good actor, too, because he does humor that revolves around life, a good slice of life.

JOAN RIVERS ON WOODY ALLEN:
I was jealous as hell of Woody. Terribly jealous that the New York intellectuals were beginning to make a big fuss over him and then would leave the Duplex [comedy club] before I came on.

LARRY KING ON WOODY ALLEN:
I think Woody's monologues, some of which are preserved on records, hold up

better today than the work of any other comedian of that time.

DICK CAVETT ON WOODY ALLEN:
I got there [Blue Angel club] just as the lights went down and he came on. His opening jokes were marvelous. They were not formula; they showed complex intelligence and genuine wit. It was marvelous just to see this high level sustained throughout his act, instead of the intermittent gems of good but lesser comics…I recognized immediately that there was no young comedian in the country who was in the same class with him for sheer brilliance of jokes…

WOODY ALLEN ON MORT SAHL:
He was absolutely like nothing anybody had ever seen before…each joke he made was not just a golf joke, for instance, but a genuine insight into politics, into social relationships between men and women… The whole face of comedy changed completely.

MORT SAHL ON WOODY ALLEN:
To this day [Woody] maintains that my conversational manner influenced his own comedy stylings. In fact, he says I impacted not only his career, but his life. That's hefty praise coming from anyone, not to mention one of the greatest comedic wits of our time.

SHELLEY BERMAN ON MORT SAHL:
He was a major inspiration because he showed me that *humor* will sell, not stand-up

jokes. I was a fourth-wall actor. You get up and do your thing and you don't talk to the audience. So I wangled an audition at Mister Kelly's, and I got up there on a stool and I made a little phone call and the audience screamed.

GEORGE CARLIN ON LENNY BRUCE:
The breadth and depth of imagination just struck me as being—I mean this was like Magellan and Columbus...this was all brand new territory.

DICK GREGORY:
Mort Sahl was one of the most influential comics out there. He was an intellect, not a genius. I looked around and there was Lenny Bruce...he was a genius. So I had one white comic over here, he's more intellectual than me; another white comic over here, he's a genius; so I go back to Bob Hope. So here I was inside a black body, influenced by white men in my head.

WOODY ALLEN ON LENNY BRUCE:
I was not a great fan of his. Now, I think he was very good, but he didn't mean much to me personally. I adored Mort Sahl, I adored Mike Nichols and Elaine May, and I adored Jonathan Winters...I found [Bruce] talented, but pretentious...I think he was a good and talented comedian, but nowhere near in the class of these others.

MORT SAHL ON LENNY BRUCE:
He and I were working together, and he was a very, very warm guy. We came along and broke a few of the rules...He wanted to be a comedian, and he was one of the best.

Dick Martin on Lenny Bruce:
Not many people know this, but Lenny Bruce was our first writer and I think his influence is still being felt everywhere on the stage today.

Richard Lewis on Lenny Bruce:
He turned comedy on its ass. An amazing artist, he knew his craft better than most, of anyone who's ever worked as a comedian—and certainly the most courageous of all time. He broke the mold.

Robert Klein on Lenny Bruce:
Way ahead of his time. In the late '50s he was doing bits about racism in America in a nightclub comedic text. He was being funny about it too, not preachy.

I as a practitioner and everyone else owes him a tremendous amount of gratitude. He took the hits.

Lenny Bruce on Lenny Bruce:
I started out as a guy being funny, but ended up having to fight for the rights of everyone.

Richard Pryor:
I'd never heard anything like him before, especially his bit about the kid who went to the hobby shop to buy airplane glue, but was afraid to ask for it. Instead he asked for everything else, all sort of crap, one item after another. Finally, after he'd gotten everything else, he blurted out that he also wanted something like two thousand tubes of glue. That destroyed me...And in my mind, nobody, to this day, has made an

album as brilliantly funny as Lenny Bruce's *Lima, Ohio*.

STEVE MARTIN ON BOB NEWHART:
There are three guys you have to lump together: Lenny Bruce, Bob Newhart, Shelley Berman. But Newhart was very important. He was like this new thing. During his stand-up act, he didn't deliver his material. It was just this really relaxed attitude. In a way, Newhart started the era of standup comedian.

JACK BENNY ON WOODY ALLEN:
I don't know anyone who is as clever and funny and has the knowledge of what to do in his writing and acting as Woody. No one compares with him. I used to say these things about Ed Wynn. My wife wouldn't sit next to me when I watched him because I made a fool of myself. Now I sit alone and scream at Woody.

LARRY KING ON WOODY ALLEN:
I think Woody's monologues, so many of which are preserved on records, hold up better today than the work of any other comedian of that time.

GARRY MARSHALL ON NICHOLS & MAY:
Mike Nichols and Elaine May invented entire casts of characters onstage right before the audience's eyes. Their comedy was almost an extension of the cerebral approach: they would take a concept, character, or prop and experiment with it to see where it would take them.

CATHY LADMAN ON NICHOLS & MAY:
> In 1989, I was in my apartment, getting ready to do my very first appearance on *The Tonight Show*. I thought I'd put on some music so I could sing and work with all the adrenaline that was pumping through my system. And, all of a sudden, it occurred to me to put on *Nichols and May Examine Doctors*. And there I was, about to fulfill a comedian's dream by going on *The Tonight Show*, and listening to the very thing that first inspired me. It was the sweetest moment of my life.

BILLY CRYSTAL ON JONATHAN WINTERS:
> My parents would let me stay up late to watch Jack Paar when Jonathan Winters was on. He was my favorite.

ROBIN WILLIAMS ON JONATHAN WINTERS:
> Jonathan transforms himself. He's like Buddha meets Gumby...Having him on [*Mork & Mindy*] was one of the main reasons I stayed with it. For me, it was a chance to play alongside Babe Ruth. I'd always wanted just to meet Winters. When I was a kid, my parents would say, 'all right, you can stay up a little longer to watch this wonderful man fly around the room and do all this crazy stuff."

BOB NEWHART ON JONATHAN WINTERS:
> I went to see Johnny at the Black Orchid in Chicago. And I was just starting out...And I watched him for an hour. He was hilarious. Each joke was funnier than the one before it. I was totally discouraged. And I thought, why bother? I mean, that's the funniest

man in the world. Why would you even think of going into the field of comedy? There's no way you can be as funny as Jonathan Winters.

STEVE ALLEN ON JONATHAN WINTERS:
Probably a fraction of 1% of Jonathan funniest moments in life have been captured on film.

DICK GREGORY: Humor can no more find the solution to race problems than it can cure cancer. We didn't laugh Hitler out of existence.

JOAN RIVERS ON DICK GREGORY:
The anger and bitterness in him were so great, you could see he would not last long as a comic. He could not keep himself from making a statement—and you cannot make statements through comedy. Your anger can be forty-nine percent and your comedy fifty-one percent, and you are okay. If the anger is fifty-one percent, the comedy is gone. Comedy is anger, but anger is not comedy.

LILY TOMLIN ON JOAN RIVERS:
I go back with Joan to the Downstairs, when she was already famous. I was in the review Upstairs. I used to come down the back stairs when I wasn't on and watch her through a crack in the door. I'd be literally laughing so hard I had to stifle myself not to be a real distraction.

HENNY YOUNGMAN ON JOAN RIVERS:
She has a natural talent. She knows what's funny. I'm tough to make laugh and she makes me laugh.

GARRY MARSHALL ON JOEY BISHOP:
> While many of the other comics yelled onstage, sweated, and pounded out their material, Joey was different. He didn't want the audiences to hear his act. He wanted them to overhear his material. He wanted material he could present in a casual, cute way that looked like he had just made it up.

JACK BENNY ON JOEY BISHOP:
> He's one of the funniest men I have ever seen. He's just naturally a funny man. Great ad-lib comedian…thinks fast.

STEVE ALLEN ON BILL COSBY:
> Bill Cosby is nothing less than the most gifted monologist of our time.

BRAD GARRETT ON BILL COSBY:
> Cosby was huge for me. Huge!

ROBERT KLEIN ON RODNEY DANGERFIELD:
> He's one of the finest joke writers of all time. In a league with Neil Simon. He's a natural. He's a character for America.

JOAN RIVERS ON RODNEY DANGERFIELD:
> I do not like him [personally], but tell me he is playing somewhere and I will get dressed and run to see him. I have *tremendous* respect for Rodney as a comic—he has the most brilliant, the most inventive, the meanest humor—and he makes a fool of himself. There is a lot of me in Rodney and vice versa.

ROSEANNE ON RODNEY DANGERFIELD:
> I love Rodney Dangerfield. He's so unbelievably dark. And so sad. He'll get

real intense, get right into your face. Outta his mind comes the truest, meanest things in the world.

JACKIE MASON ON RODNEY DANGERFIELD:
He studied every routine down to the second, he practiced every word, every gesture, marched up and down, trying out the jokes. He wouldn't take a Carson show more than every six weekends because it takes him that long to make every word perfect. It had to be timed exactly, word for word, that he was going to do six minutes on the spot, three minutes on the couch.

THE '60S AND BEYOND

SHELLEY BERMAN: There was a time I guess in America [when] we got more overtly rebellious. I think it had to do with the Vietnam War, and with the Supreme Court saying blacks were equal, and the blacks kept saying, 'okay, when?'...and we had kids on campuses rebelling and people started screaming—and music got louder, and poetry got raunchier, and comedy got extremely hostile. And you can't really be entirely subtle when you're being hostile...we did, as a result, lose our subtleties.

STEVE MARTIN: It had to do with making people laugh at something other than punchlines. People called it "anti-comedy." There was a period in the late '60s and early '70s when you could just mention the word "Nixon" and get a huge laugh. Everybody was angry. The comedians were angry, the audience was angry. I knew the war was coming to an end, and I thought that we had been angry long enough. I was the first person on the scene to be apolitical. I didn't want to talk about Vietnam or Watergate. I just wanted to be funny.

JERRY SEINFELD ON ROBERT KLEIN:
The father of '80s comedy. I think 90% of the comedians you watch today are imitating Klein in some form or another, myself included.

JAY LENO ON ROBERT KLEIN:
If I had one major influence, it was Klein. His background seemed similar to mine. Just a guy raised by a normal middle-class family. His points of reference were the same as mine: current television, pop culture, mass media, and the ridiculous details of a young person's everyday life. And this was a revelation to me.

PAUL REISER ON ROBERT KLEIN:
Robert had a big influence on all of us. He just brought stand-up to a very accessible level. It was hip and now. He created language that wasn't there before.

DAVID BRENNER ON ROBERT KLEIN:
I thought his mind was brilliant. Robert Klein was one of the great "acting" comics. Like Richard Pryor, he got into the characters and made them come alive. I thought he was going to be what Robin Williams became. I don't know what happened.

ROBERT KLEIN: I'm a good act. But I let myself wither on the vine.

DAMON WAYANS ON RICHARD PRYOR:
If [a comedian] hasn't copied from Richard Pryor, then you're probably not funny. Like Michael Jordan has defined the game of basketball, Richard Pryor has defined stand-up comedy.

ROBIN WILLIAMS ON RICHARD PRYOR:
When he kicks there is no one in the world better. No one has ever done what he does. He is the king of that…And his stand-up, he sets the rules. Then he destroyed the boundaries.

EDDIE MURPHY ON RICHARD PRYOR:
As a teenager when I watched Richard Pryor for the first time, I realized what I was—a comedian. He paints pictures with words. He can tell you a story and you can see the whole thing. He was a genius.

DICK GREGORY ON RICHARD PRYOR:
These young comedians grew up in a time where everybody wanted to be like Richard Pryor, but without realizing that his genius had nothing to do with his profanity. He never used profanity as a punchline. If you go back and bleeped all of the profanity out of Richard Pryor's stuff, it is still hilarious. His genius outweighed the profanity.

LILY TOMLIN ON RICHARD PRYOR:
When I saw Richard working, I just loved it so much. I felt I saw into the heart of him. Nobody else was doing it. I was so gratified

to be moved on that level, the way he would perform those little moments. It's not just the material, it's the whole marriage of the sensibility and someone's own humanity.

JAY LENO ON GEORGE CARLIN:
George Carlin was my favorite when I as a kid. He had a whole hour where he just talked about things he used to do in school—passing notes, throwing spitballs, etc. I really loved listening to it, because he talked about a lot of things I did.

ROBIN WILLIAMS:
I couldn't find any acting work. But I needed to perform, so I started doing stand-up. After a while you realize that Juilliard training is a tool. The ability to project and enunciate worked great, even in comedy clubs, because I wouldn't use a microphone, and I had a voice that could kick the crap out of the back of the room.

BILLY CRYSTAL ON ROBIN WILLIAMS:
No one else comes even close to being so powerful, so explosive.

MICHAEL RICHARDS ON ANDY KAUFMAN:
I loved Andy. He could fool people. He was a great trickster. I knew exactly what he was up to, and I did a lot of that myself before I even met Andy and saw his work.

JIM CARREY ON ANDY KAUFMAN:
Andy was a person who opened his eyes in the morning, and the circus began. He never got nervous about being on a television show; he thought they were silly. He didn't all of a sudden [go] into character. He arrived

as the character; he was the character. He was so committed, in fact, that people thought he was sick.

CARL REINER ON ANDY KAUFMAN:
He's playing a game and he's enjoying the game. But we're not enjoying it as much as he is...Unless you let the audience in on the joke, you are making fools of them...He has to tell them, somehow, 'I'm going to do the worst act in the world, and the game we're playing is to see how long you can take it before you bomb me.' At least then there's an audience catharsis, even if it's anger instead of laughter. But they have to know why they're angry or laughing.

STEVE MARTIN:
I feel I am the link for the normal audience to understand Andy Kaufman. Andy is where I may have gone if [my act] never worked.

ANDY KAUFMAN:
I am *not* a comic. I have never told a joke. I don't even watch comedians nowadays...I can manipulate people's reactions. There are different kinds of laughter. Gut laughter used to happen from what I did. Gut laughter is where you don't have a choice, you've got to laugh. Gut laughter doesn't come from the intellect. And it's much harder for me to evoke now, because I'm known. They say, "Oh, wow, Andy Kaufman, he's a really funny guy." But I'm not trying to be funny. I just want to play with their heads.

RICHARD LEWIS ON ELAINE BOOSLER:
She was the Jackie Robinson of my generation. She was the strongest female working. She broke the mold for most female comics.

BILLY CRYSTAL ON EDDIE MURPHY:
I don't think he's a good comedian. I think he's a wonderful actor and a fine sketch player and characterizer.

BILLY CRYSTAL ON SAM KINISON:
Kinison has something to say, both outrageous and funny, within the yelling. It's not a gimmick. He screams his lungs out because that's what he really believes. He's saying that something is wrong.

CHRIS ROCK ON SAM KINISON:
I try to be Sam Kinison, comedically. I just remember Sam Kinison, when I was coming up, was the only guy who sounded new. Everybody else was doing different versions of other guys. Even Eddie [Murphy] did Pryor, Pryor kind of did Cosby. Jerry Seinfeld did Robert Klein. I don't know anybody that sounds like Sam Kinison.

DAN AYKROYD:
We laugh at toilet jokes, at shock. Then you get into the Nineties and you have guys like Sam Kinison, God rest his soul, and Andrew Dice Clay—the abrasive and caustic humorists. That's really what has changed. It's like everything is through the top now and we have people out there who are striving to shock. I don't know what [that future] will bring. Maybe guys will be chopping their fingers off.

JANEANE GAROFALO:
See, I don't know where [my] reputation comes from. Whenever I do my stand-up, and I criticize something, I bend over backward to be as diplomatic as I can. So, when people categorize me as angry or sarcastic

or sharp, I really don't know what they're talking about. I think maybe I appear aggressive in the way that I present myself, but it's certainly not intentional.

STEVE MARTIN: When you look over the decades, from the '50s to the '90s, there are probably only six or seven comics who stood out and could be called artists...Newhart, Cosby, Pryor, Eddie Murphy, Jim Carrey. Certainly George Carlin. They're kind of obvious choices.

BILLY CRYSTAL: A comedian says things that are really human. A comic comes out and pulls down his pants and says, 'Look I got a rubber duck here!' That's why I love Lily Tomlin, Richard Pryor, and Albert Brooks. Their stuff is about something. When I start feeling like I'm a comic is when I stop doing it.

THE BIG PAYOFF

JACKIE GLEASON: I was in a graduation play in grammar school, and I got a laugh. That laugh... was the greatest thing that could possibly happen to you. And if you could go out in front of an audience, and do things that make them happy and make them laugh...there's no greater thrill.

BILL COSBY: I used to want to destroy people with laughter. I wanted to make their stomachs hurt. But that isn't fair. It really hurts and it makes people tired. So now I pace myself. I don't want people concentrating on their pain rather than their laughter.

George Carlin: When I was young, I used to resent the fact that certain comedians would get laughs the moment they reached the stage, and I had to fight 20 minutes to get the same audience on my side. It takes a long time to earn that respect, and now I appreciate it.

George Burns: Believe me, there is nothing that feels as good as standing onstage and hearing the laughter and applause of an audience. Nothing.

Rodney Dangerfield: The joy for me doing stand-up is, more so than any other medium in show business—I mean, television, movies—stand-up is the only place you can have a romance with the audience. Boom, the rhythm's going, they're laughing, you're knocking them out...Can't do that in television, movies, nothing. That's how show business started, in English music halls. Live is the only way.

Lenny Bruce: I'm at my best when they let me be silly—I mean zany—nuts. If they think I'm funny, I think, "Boy, these are my people, they think like Lenny Bruce." Then I'm really going to show off for them—I really feel a love for them.

Chevy Chase: Stand-up comics are a breed of comedian that live with rejection. They almost strive for rejection year after year. And when they finally receive notice and attention and adulation, it's overwhelming...A stand-up comedian is willing to make a fool of himself to get recognition, and when he gets it, he's thrown into a world where they're no perspective for a while. And it's dangerous.

Rodney Dangerfield: You do whatever you feel will get the biggest response. I wanna get as many laughs as I can.

Caroline Rhea: If you're lucky enough to find the essence of who you are—and if you're a comedian, it's that you're funny—it's the only time where you feel fully and totally alive, is when you're doing it and blissfully happy in front of strangers that you're making laugh—more so than any other time. Much more so than a one-on-one conversation...It's the response you get, and the sort of dance that you do that's so much more fulfilling.

Henny Youngman: Now, more than ever, after sixty-plus years onstage, I never feel so young, so alive, so happy, as when I'm making people laugh.

From Stand-Ups to Sitcoms

Ray Romano: Every day I'm in the writers' room. Every story, every line...we collaborate together. All of us...I wrote four scripts already myself with a partner, but it's so hard. It's the hardest thing I've ever done, writing a script from scratch. I'd never experienced that. I think it's hard writing a segue for one of my jokes! Trying to write a whole scene with dialogue, ugh! But it was a great feeling to do it. As a stand-up, the hardest part for me is to accept someone else's material, you kook me a while to get over that. What a great feeling it is to write the script yourself so you're not only performing in a sitcom, but it's your material too. I really got a kick out of that.

JEFF FOXWORTHY: [The writers] didn't want a whole lot of input from me. I wasn't even allowed in the writing room for the first half of the first year. And that was frustrating, 'cause I said, you know I've been on the road doing five hundred shows a year. I know what works for me.

MARGARET CHO: The executives were the most humorless, dry, intimidating people I had ever met. They were the kind of people in an audience who wince instead of laugh. We were trying to talk about comedy, but nobody laughed once in the meeting. I had bad feelings about them all; they didn't seem very nice. But they wanted to do this show, this Asian-American sitcom, and they wanted me to star in it.

RAY ROMANO: The stand-up comedians who make it [on television] I think are the ones that have a personality and are relatable on stage. There are some stand-ups who are doing characters on stage, but Roseanne is Roseanne, and Tim Allen is Tim Allen on stage, and they translate it into stand-up. They're having a conversation onstage with you, you see who they are in the stand up. And why not build a show around that?

JERRY SEINFELD: This show is about comedy. It's not about characters. It's not about people's lives. It's just about what's funny. That's what determines the storylines. We are sometimes just a thin layer above a sketch show.

Carol Leifer: The greatest thing about having worked on *Seinfeld* was that I came to appreciate small ideas, because to me those are the funniest.

Carl Reiner on Jerry Seinfeld:
Jerry Seinfeld is a straight man in the Great Straight Man tradition. They have to know where the jokes are and not to step on them. Bud Abbott was brilliant. George Burns too.

Seinfeld has got the Jack Benny syndrome. On his show, he's the pivotal point like Jack Benny was. But the people who got the big laughs on the Jack Benny show were Phil Harris and Rochester. In this case, [the supporting actors] are all better actors than Seinfeld. They are probably the four most dysfunctional people in the history of television comedy.

Ellen DeGeneres: I'll be the first to admit I definitely want acceptance. It's why I went into comedy—comedians for some reason lacked enough attention growing up...I have a tendency to diminish what I do for a living but I also know I'm going to leave here, and I won't be somebody who just had a sitcom but someone who helped change people's minds.

Whoopi Goldberg: Now we've got whole networks that have essentially been built on black programming, even though the programming kind of sets us back. Now we're back to the eye-poppin', slang slingin' shit we used to get from J.J. on *Good Times*, when we should be beyond that. I'm sorry, but Martin Lawrence does not reflect what it means to be black today any more than Beaver and Wally reflected what it meant to be white in 1960.

CHRIS ROCK: Humor really transcends everything. My whole family loves Rodney Dangerfield. And I don't know a white person that didn't laugh at Redd Foxx or *The Jeffersons*.

COMEDIANS FACE-TO-FACE

CHARLIE CHAPLIN TO GROUCHO MARX:
I wish I could talk on screen the way you do.

TED HEALY TO MILTON BERLE:
Milton, there's no such thing as an old joke. If you haven't heard it before, it's new.

W.C. FIELDS TO JACK BENNY:
I never miss your show and it seems that I appreciate it all the more with every broadcast. I feel that I am in with you and Mary and Rochester…and it is something to look forward to on Sunday evening.

W. C. FIELDS (LETTER TO MACK SENNETT):
Mack, I do not wish to run your studio or change one idea you have. You have been a tremendous success with your formula, but it is new to me and I can't change my way of working at this late stage of the game. When I have the stage all set for a Fields

picture and you come in and have everything changed for a Sennett picture, you see how you have rendered me helpless. You told me I would get screen credit for the stories I wrote and that I could do as I wished until I went wrong. If the pictures made are not what you want, tear up the contract. You know I would never hold you to a piece of paper. We are friends.

MILTON BERLE TO JACKIE GLEASON (TO BE GUEST ON BERLE'S TV SHOW):
You bastard, you are going to rehearse with me all week. None of this no-show-until-airtime stuff with me.

GROUCHO MARX TO FRED ALLEN:
You are the best humorist of our time, and still you don't do a Goddamed thing about it. Of all the millions of books, good, bad, and otherwise, there isn't one by Fred Allen. I have lectured you about this time and time again and I will continue to do so until you capitulate.

STAN LAUREL TO DICK VAN DYKE:
If anybody ever decides to do a film on my life, I would like you to play me. (Years later, van Dyke said, "It was the greatest complement I ever had in my life.")

DICK GREGORY TO BILLY CRYSTAL:
You are one entertaining cat.

JONATHAN WINTERS TO ROBIN WILLIAMS:
Don't call me your mentor. People back in Ohio don't know what that means. Call me your idol.

GROUCHO MARX TO DICK CAVETT:
> I watched you on the Merv Griffin show and you came off very well. I think you could now take a chance and stop writing jokes for other people. Write them for yourself....I notice you seem to be adopting some of [Woody Allen's] mannerisms. Forget it. Be yourself or you'll never get anywhere.

GROUCHO MARX TO DAN ROWAN:
> I think you're one of the greatest straight men I've ever seen. There has never been a good comedian that didn't have a good straight man.

JOHNNY CARSON TO ROSEANNE:
> You're going to be a big star, maybe the biggest woman comic ever. I personally guarantee it.

Chapter 9
Comedians as Actors

Hal Roach: The great comedians imitate children. To be a great comedian you have to be a great actor, and to be a great actor you have to portray something. There is not a great visual actor that I know whose every movement is not that of a child...When you take a grown person, and do the same thing as you would do with a child, it becomes just as amusing. And that is the basis of so-called slapstick comedy.

Jack Benny: The trick in playing comedy is to make an audience believe what is going on and for this you have to believe it first yourself. This is why think a comedian is basically an actor. The art of comedy is like the art of acting—except that in comedy, the actor has to be able to believe the most preposterous and exaggerated things.

Shelley Berman on Jack Benny:
If you remember *To Be or Not To Be*, then you will remember a fine, *elegant* acting performance from a man entirely convinced of his circumstance, and working with all the good rules. He was splendid.

JOHNNY CARSON ON JACK BENNY:
> He was a marvelous actor. If you go look at *To Be or Not To Be*, you'll find that he was a fine comedy actor.

RED BUTTONS ON ED WYNN:
> When he had a chance to do it, Ed Wynn was a wonderful, wonderful actor in the twilight of his career.

W.C. FIELDS ON FANNIE BRICE:
> Fannie Brice—"Baby Snooks," comical dancer, comedienne, did Burlesque dances, sang character songs in Yiddish and other dialects—she was a fine dramatic actress. Believe it or prove your ignorance.

GARRY MARSHALL ON JACKIE GLEASON:
> Jackie Gleason was mostly known as a comedian from TV but he was also a heck of an actor and did some wonderful work in films, and probably did not receive enough accolades as an actor.

SHELLEY BERMAN: I could name just a few [comedians as good actors], and whenever I am asked to name them, I have named Jackie Gleason, as an actor; I remember Jack Benny being a beautiful actor, and the other beautiful actor who's a comedian is Red Buttons.

GEORGE BURNS: Good acting is when Walter Matthau says to me, 'How are you?' and if I answer 'Fine,' that's good acting. If Walter Matthau asks me 'How are you?' and I answer 'I think it fell on the floor,' then that's bad acting.

Jonathan Winters: A lot of people who've seen me do a couple of dramatic things come up to me and say, "I didn't know you could act—I thought you only made noises." They forget that all of us can act; what else are we doing up there?

Dan Rowan: I'm an actor, and that's *all* I am. I have the ability to think and write comedy and I can act comedy, too, but I have done and intend to do straight things that have no humor at all attached to them.

Rodney Dangerfield: Comedy is much harder than drama, even though it doesn't seem that way. There are many comedians who are great actors, but there are no great actors who are comedians.

Carol Burnett: I have seen comedians switch over to drama with greater success than I have seen straight actors switch to comedy. Straight actors who aren't really comedic force something too much.

Bill Murray: It may sound funny, but [dramatic roles] are fun. They're important, because they let people see another side of you. I think comedy's a little harder. To play comedy, you have to be able to play straight. The way you modulate it and deliver it is what makes it become funny—but you have to be able to play straight.

Gene Wilder: Comedy is hard—if you're not a comic actor. And drama is hard if you're not a dramatic actor. Some actors are blessed with the talent to be good in both—Spencer Tracy and Cary Grand, for example. I wish

I were blesses that way, but I'll never be as good in drama as I am in comedy.

JANEANE GAROFALO: There are a lot of comics who make great actors, like Robin Williams. When he's not trying too hard, he's wonderful, and Jim Carrey's very good. Nora Dunn is a good actor. Garry Shandling. So it can be very natural. And then there are some comedians who aren't very good because they can't stop trying for the laugh.

MILTON BERLE: In a straight role there's no going after laughs, no pauses or waiting— 'if this is supposed to be funny shall I take three beats?' It is much more difficult to be funny and to get laughs..."

ROSCOE "FATTY" ARBUCKLE:
I know one thing. I'd a heap rather make people laugh than make 'em cry. It's a darned sight harder to do. Sometimes I think I've picked out the worst job in sight. If you don't believe me, try to be funny for thirty solid minutes yourself. After that you'll want to be a villain or a vampire just by way of a little relaxation.

JACKIE GLEASON: I have known many comedians—Berle is one—who were superb in serious drama, but there are very few serious actors who do comedy well. Cary Grant, William Powell— especially Powell in *My Man Godfrey*—and Jack Lemmon are among the few.

JACK LEMMON ON MILTON BERLE:
If I was a director, I wouldn't hesitate to hire him for a very good, strong dramatic

part. The only reason I haven't is because Milton would tell me how to direct it.

GROUCHO MARX: There's is hardly a comedian alive who isn't capable of doing a first-rate dramatic role. But there are mighty few dramatic actors who could essay a comic role with any distinction...All first-rate comedians who have played dramatic roles are almost unanimous in saying that compared to being funny, dramatic acting is like a two-week vacation in the country.

JERRY LEWIS: The hard job is doing comedy. That's what's rough. Acting is a snap, but acting for an *actor* is hard work...because that's all he does. It *is* like two weeks in the country. Christ, that's a pleasure, and easy...that's nowhere as naked as being a comedian.

Chapter 10
In Closing...

Steve Allen: I have discovered the important rules of comedy—about 4,000 of them.

Milton Berle: Every comedian, every comic, every funny woman, every funny man is a hero—because what they can do for society and for the world no one else can do, and that's to make people laugh.

Roseanne Barr: Comics are the greatest damn people on earth, never really too secure.

Fred Allen: All that a comedian has to show for his years of work and aggravation is the echo of forgotten laughter.

Red Skelton: When the show's over, I walk into this empty auditorium. And there's no applause, there's no echo of laughter, and I say to myself, "An hour ago, I was important. Tomorrow I must start again."

BIBLIOGRAPHY

BOOKS:

Allen, Fred. *Much Ado About Me*. New York: Little, Brown & Company, 1956.

Allen, Fred. *Treadmill to Oblivion*. New York: Little, Brown & Company, 1954.

Allen, Woody and Stig Bjorkman. *Woody Allen on Woody Allen*. New York: Grove Press, 1993.

Bacon, James. *How Sweet It Is*. New York: St. Martin's Press, 1985.

Ball, Lucille, with Betty Hannah Hoffman. *Love, Lucy*. New York: G.P. Putnam's Sons, 1986.

Benny, Jack and Joan Benny. *Sunday Nights at Seven*. New York: Warner Books, 1990.

Borns, Betsy. *Comic Lives: Inside the World of Stand-up Comedy*. New York: Fireside/Simon & Schuster, 1987

Cahn, William and Rhoda Cahn. *The Great American Comedy Scene*. New York: Monarch, 1978.

Campbell, Robert. *The Golden Years of Broadcasting*. New York: Rutledge Books, 1976.

Cantor, Eddie. *The Way I See It.* Englewood Cliffs, NJ. Prentice-Hall, 1959.

Chaplin, Charles. *My Autobiography.* Random House UK, 1964.

Crystal, Billy, with Dick Schaap. *Absolutely Mahvelous.* New York: G.P. Putnam's Sons, 1986.

Dangerfield, Rodney. *It's Not Easy Bein' Me.* New York: HarperCollins, 2004.

Deschner, Donald. *The Films of W.C. Fields.* Secaucus, N.J.: Citadel Press, 1966.

Edmonds, Andy. *Frame Up!.* New York: Avon Books, 1991.

Emery, Robert J. *The Directors: Take Two.* New York: TV Books, 2000.

Fields, Ronald. *W.C. Fields: A Life on Film.* New York: St. Martin's Press, 1984.

Fields, Ronald (editor). *W.C. Fields by Himself.* Englewood Cliffs, NJ: Prentice-Hall, 1973.

Gallo, Hank. *Comedy Explosion: A New Generation.* New York: Thunder's Mouth Press, 1991.

King, Alan, with Chris Chase. *Name-dropping: The Life and Lies of Alan King.* New York: Touchstone/Simon & Shuster, 1996.

Kramer, Stanley with Thomas M. Coffey. *A Mad, Mad, Mad, Mad World.* New York: Harcourt Brace & Company, 1997.

Leno, Jay. *Leading With My Chin.* New York: HarperCollins, 1996.

Marshall, Garry, with Lori Marshall. *Wake Me When It's Funny.* New York: Newmarket Press, 1995.

Marx, Groucho. *Groucho and Me.* New York: Bernard Geis Associates, 1959.

Marx, Groucho. *The Groucho Letters.* New York: Manor Books, 1967.

Marx, Groucho and Richard J. Anobile. *The Marx Brothers Scrapbook.* New York: Grosset & Dunlap, 1974.

Marx, Harpo, with Rowland Barber. *Harpo Speaks!* New York: Freeway Press, 1974.

Mason Jackie, with Ken Gross. *Jackie, Oy!:* Jack Mason from Birth to Rebirth. New York: Little Brown & Co., 1988.

McCabe, John. *Mr. Laurel & Mr. Hardy.* New York: Grosset & Dunlap, 1961, 1966.

McCabe, John and Al Kilgore and Richard W. Bann. *Laurel & Hardy.* New York: E.P. Dutton, 1975.

McGovern, Edythe. *Not-So-Simple Neil Simon: A Critical Study.* Van Nuys, CA: Perivale Press, 1978.

Morgan, Robert (editor). *Stand-Up Comedians on Television.* New York: The Museum of Television & Radio/ Harry N. Abrams, Inc. 1996.

Morgan, David (editor). *Monty Python Speaks.* New York: Avon Books, 1999.

Newhart, Bob. *I Shouldn't Even Be Doing This!* New York: Hyperion, 2006.

Parish, James Robert and William T. Leonard. *The Funsters.* New Rochelle, N.Y.: Arlington House, 1979.

Rico, Donna. *Kovacs Land.* New York: Harcout Brace Jovanovich, 1990.

Rivers, Joan, with Richard Meryman. *Still Talking*. Turtle Bay Books/Random House, 1991.

Stone, Laurie. *Laughing in the Dark: A Decade of Subversive Comedy*. Hopewell, NJ: The Ecco Press., 1997.

Taylor, Robert. *Fred Allen: His Life and Wit*. New York: Little, Brown and Company, 1989.

Terkel, Studs. *The Studs Terkel Interviews—Film and Theatre*. New York: The New Press, 1999.

Waldron, Vince. *Classic Sitcoms*. New York: Collier Books, 1987.

Walker, Jay. *The Leno Wit*. New York: Adler and Robin Books, Inc., 1997.

Welles, Orson, and Peter Bogdonovich. *This is Orson Welles*. New York: Harper Collins, 1992.

Wilde, Larry. *The Great Comedians Talk About Comedy*, Secaucus, N.J.: Citadel Press, 1968.

Wilder, Gene. *Kiss Me Like A Stranger: My Search For Love and Art*. New York: St. Martin's Press, 2006.

Young, Jordan R. *The Laugh Crafters*. New York: G.P. Putnam's Sons, 1996.

Newspapers/Magazines:

George Burns quote "good acting/bad acting": *New York Times*, February 27, 1976 "George Burns at Carnegie: Remembrance of Gags Past"

Chevy Chase letter to editor re: Groucho: *NY Times*, Sunday, October 9, 1977

Blake Edwards on Peter Sellers: *NY Times*, 1976.

Robert Klein on Dangerfield "greatest joke writer": *Rolling Stone*, September 18, 1980; Dangerfield quote, "I wanna get as many laughs as I can," ibid.

Milton Berle on comedy: *USA Today*, August 1st, 1984.

Mort Sahl: "A lot of rules...it's as simple as that" *Chicago Tribune*, The Arts, April 20, 1986; J. Seinfeld, "100% conviction," ibid.

Milton Berle: "Of course it's an art form..." *New York* magazine June 19, 1995

Seinfeld on Klein: "Father of 80s comedy" *Comedy USA* Vol.2 No.1, July 1987

Roach on Lloyd: "played a comedian" *NY Times* January 22, 1992.

TELEVISION DOCUMENTARIES:

"The Great Stand-Ups." Produced by Stuart Smiley, Robert B. Weide, in assoc. with HBO, c. 1984.

A&E Biography: Sid Caesar. Produced by Del Jack & Cress Darwin, c.1994 Millenial Entertainment Inc. in association with A&E.

A & E Biography: Steve Allen. "Hi Ho, Steverino!" same credits as above

"Jack Benny: 'Love In Bloom' " Irving Fein, Executive Producer. HBO c. 1992.

"Influences – The Museum of Television and Radio". Produced by Christine Triano, Robert Batscha, Jean-Michel Michenaud, and Chris Cowan, c.2000.

American Masters: "Alan King's College of Comedy." PBS, 1997–2001

American Masters: "Neil Simon: Not Just For Laughs." Executive Producer Susan Lacy, Produced by Manya Starr. WNET 1989.

"Caesar's Writers" PBS, 1996.

American Masters: "Vaudeville" Produced by Rosemary Garner. Production of WNET, KCTS/9 Television, and Palmer/Fenster. 1997

INDEX

A
Abbott & Costello, 2, 51, 52
Agee, James, 33, 35, 38
Allen, Fred, 19, 20, 27, 28, 45-48, 111, 119
Allen, Gracie, 26
Allen, Steve, 1, 5, 11, 18, 26, 42, 46, 66-68, 90, 98
Allen, Woody, 32, 39, 52, 53, 60, 61, 91-92, 93, 95
Amsterdam, Morey, 89
Arbuckle, Roscoe "Fatty," 10, 29, 30, 55, 116
Aykroyd, Dan, 10, 31, 104

B
Ball, Lucille, 8, 15, 41, 63, 64
Barr, Roseanne, 98, 112, 119
Belushi, John, 69
Belzer, Richard, 87, 88
Benny, Jack, 3, 8, 13, 24, 27, 46, 61-63, 81, 95, 110, 113, 114
Berle, Milton, 3, 6, 15, 20, 22, 27, 57, 58, 68, 80, 86, 90, 110, 111, 116, 119
Berman, Shelley, 3, 91, 92, 99, 113, 114
Bergen, Edgar, 49
Bishop, Joey, 98

Bob & Ray, 49
Boosler, Elaine, 103
Brecher, Irving, 40, 46
Brenner, David, 81, 83, 100
Brice, Fanny, 12, 23, 114
Brooks, Albert, 31, 62
Brooks, Mel, 9, 33, 54, 56, 60, 61
Bruce, Lenny, 6, 83, 91, 93, 94, 106
Burnett, Carol, 7, 51, 61, 66, 69, 115
Burns, George, 8, 14, 21, 26, 28, 41, 45-47, 89, 106
Butler, Brett, 77, 84, 88
Buttons, Red, 90

C
Caesar, Sid, 6, 23, 57, 58, 69
Candy, John, 8
Cantor, Eddie, 21, 22, 24, 42, 46
Carlin, George, 93, 102, 106
Carney, Art, 57
Carrey, Jim, 15, 53, 54, 102
Carson, Johnny, 71-72, 83, 112, 114
Carter, Jack, 22
Cavett, Dick, 38, 47, 67, 92, 112
Chaplin, Charlie, 20, 30-32, 35, 37, 110
Chase, Charlie, 35
Chase, Chevy, 12, 24, 65, 69, 106
Cho, Margaret, 85, 108

Clay, Andrew Dice, 83
Cleese, John, 4
Coca, Imogene, 60-61
Conway, Tim, 69
Cosby, Bill, 70, 98, 105
Costello, Lou, 42
Crystal, Billy, 35, 55, 59, 61, 77, 84, 86, 96, 102, 104, 105, 111

D
Dana, Bill, 80
Dangerfield, Rodney, 7, 79, 80, 98, 99, 106, 107, 115
Danson, Ted, 66, 67
DeGeneres, Ellen, 109
Diller, Phyllis, 6, 8, 15, 40, 87
Drescher, Fran, 63

E
Edwards, Blake, 54

F
Fields, Totie, 91
Fields, W.C., 1, 2, 3, 5, 9, 13, 22, 23, 24, 31, 37-39, 49, 110, 114
Fine, Larry, 41, 42
Foster, Phil, 76
Foxworthy, Jeff, 108

G
Garofalo, Janeane, 83, 104, 116
Garrett, Brad, 89, 98
Gelbart, Larry, 59, 61
Gervais, Ricky, 42
Gilliam, Terry, 59, 65
Gleason, Jackie, 2, 6, 7, 32, 58, 69, 105, 111, 114, 116
Gobel, George, 65
Gold, Judy, 10
Goldberg, Whoopi, 109
Greene, Shecky, 3, 89

Gregory, Dick, 93, 97, 101

H
Hackett, Buddy, 5, 78, 89
Hardy, Oliver, 13, 34
Hart, Kitty Carlisle, 40
Healy, Ted, 109
Hill, Benny, 32, 70
Hope, Bob, 25, 26, 45, 52, 93
Howard, Curly, 51
Howard, Moe, 12, 42, 51

J
Jessel, George, 26, 28
Jones, Terry, 33

K
Kaufman, Andy, 102-103
Kaye, Danny, 52
Keaton, Buster, 1, 2, 16, 29, 30-33, 35, 39, 52
King, Alan, 5, 11, 16, 26, 28, 88, 91
King, Larry, 91, 95
Kinison, Sam, 104
Klein, Robert, 94, 98, 100, 101
Korman, Harvey, 69
Kovacs, Ernie, 11, 65
Kramer, Stanley, 55

L
Ladman, Cathy, 96
Lahr, Ber, 26, 27
Laurel & Hardy, 42
Laurel, Stan, 13, 30-32, 35, 62, 63, 111
Leifer, Carol, 76, 81, 83, 109
Lemmon, Jack, 116
Leno, Jay, 11, 68, 76, 82, 84, 87, 100, 102
Leonard, Jack E., 89
Letterman, David, 66, 71, 77

Lewis, Jerry, 6, 7, 32, 52-54, 57, 67, 69, 88, 90, 117
Lewis, Richard, 75, 103
Lithgow, John, 60
Lloyd, Harold, 18, 34, 35

M
Maher, Bill, 89
Martin & Lewis, 88
Martin, Steve, 5, 6, 18
Marcau, Marcel, 64
Marshall, Garry, 56, 75, 95, 98, 114
Martin, Dick, 57, 94
Martin, Steve, 52, 63, 66, 95, 99, 103, 105
Marx Brothers, 24, 39, 40
Marx, Chico, 22
Marx, Groucho, 1, 5, 8, 13, 17, 20, 21, 23, 24, 28, 41, 53, 62, 64, 110-112, 117
Marx, Harpo, 1, 15, 19, 25, 31
Mason, Jackie, 17, 79, 86, 99
Mazurski, Paul, 52
McCarey, Leo, 34, 35, 42
Miller, Larry, 78
Murphy, Eddie, 101, 104
Murray, Bill, 18, 115
Murray, Jan 4

N
Newhart, Bob, 5, 62, 76, 78, 81, 84, 95, 96
New York Times, The, 26
Nichols & May, 95, 96

O
O'Brien, Conan, 59, 72

P
Paar, Jack, 25, 26, 48, 70
Parker, Dorothy, 4

Perelman, S.J., 57
Pryor, Richard, 59, 67, 86, 94, 101

R
Radner, Gilda, 70
Reiner, Carl, 16, 61, 66, 89, 103
Reiser, Paul, 10, 100, 109
Rhea, Caroline, 107
Richards, Michael, 4, 102
Rickels, Don, 71, 85, 89
Rivers, Joan, 17, 71, 81, 91, 97, 98
Roach, Hal, 35, 37, 113
Rock, Chris, 79, 81, 85, 104, 110
Rodriguez, Paul, 9
Rogers, Will, 21
Romano, Ray, 11, 75, 78, 107, 108
Rowan, Dan, 18, 65, 112, 115
Rudner, Rita, 78, 82

S
Sahl, Mort, 55, 85, 92, 93
Sales, Soupy, 9
Seinfeld, Jerry, 51, 62, 66, 76, 77, 80, 100, 108, 109
Sellers, Peter, 9, 53, 54
Semon, Larry, 34
Sennett, Mack, 35, 110
Sennwald, Andre, 38
Shandling, Garry, 71, 72, 80
Short, Martin, 39, 41, 53, 70
Silvers, Phil, 63
Simon, Danny, 61
Simon, Neil, 4, 6, 27
Sinbad, 83
Skelton, Red, 33, 63, 64, 119
Smothers, Dick, 82
Smothers, Tom, 65
Spielberg, Steven, 56
Stiller, Jerry, 4, 90
Steinberg, David, 57
Stewart, Jon, 73

T
Thomas, Danny, 91
Three Stooges, The, 41
Tomlin, Lilly, 67, 97, 101
Twain, Mark, 66

U
Ullman, Tracy, 60, 67, 70

V
Van Dyke, Dick, 42, 54, 66, 89, 111
Vonnegut, Kurt, 49

W
Wallace, George, 64
Wayans, Damon, 101
Welles, Orson, 23, 32, 33, 52
West, Mae, 14, 39
White, E.B., 4
Wilder, Billy, 24
Wilder, Gene, 115
Williams, Bert, 7, 9, 22
Williams, Robin, 7, 96, 101, 102, 111
Wilson, Flip, 68
Winters, Jonathan, 10, 96, 97, 111, 115
Woollcott, Alexander, 25, 39
Woulk, Herman, 48
Wynn, Ed, 3, 4, 5, 16, 17, 20, 21, 42, 114

X, Y, Z
Youngman, Henny, 19, 27, 71, 79, 81, 90, 97, 107

www.ingramcontent.com/pod-product-compliance
Lightning Source LLC
Chambersburg PA
CBHW070920160426
43193CB00011B/1534